THE ZEN TEACHING OF HUI HAI

The Zen Teaching
of Hui Hai

ON SUDDEN ILLUMINATION

*Being the Teaching of the Zen
Master Hui Hai, known as the
Great Pearl*

Rendered into English by
JOHN BLOFELD
(Chu Ch'an)

A complete translation of the Tun Wu Ju Tao Yao
Mên Lun *and of the previously unpublished* Tsung
Ching Record.

Foreword by Charles Luk

RIDER & COMPANY
London

RIDER & COMPANY
3 Fitzroy Square, London W1

An imprint of the Hutchinson Publishing Group

London Melbourne Sydney Auckland
Wellington Johannesburg Cape Town
and agencies throughout the world

First published 1962
This edition 1969
Second impression July 1973
Third impression July 1974

Printed by The Anchor Press Ltd,
and bound by Wm. Brendon & Son Ltd,
both of Tiptree, Essex
ISBN 0 09 063881 6

CONTENTS

Respectfully dedicated to that true
Buddhist, learned scholar, and author and
translator of many valuable Ch'an texts,

CHARLES LUK

FOREWORD

In the great confusion created by the publication of unauthentic versions of Mahāyāna, and particularly of Ch'an (Zen) texts, it is most gratifying to read this translation by a British scholar, Mr John Blofeld, who not only has access to the Chinese written language but also understands the profound meaning of a great Master of the Great Vehicle and of the 'Transmission' outside of Scriptures. Mr Blofeld's version in his mother tongue will clear away all unnecessary doubts and suspicions which often arise in the minds of Western Buddhists when reading the works, though authentic and genuine, of a Chinese translator.

Ch'an Master Hui Hai, known as 'the Great Pearl', was a Dharma successor to Ma Tsu, an eminent spiritual descendant of the Sixth Patriarch. The Great Pearl wrote his masterly treatise on the 'Essential Gateway to the Truth by Means of Instantaneous Awakening' which is presented in Part One of this volume. In it the Master revealed his correct interpretation of the Mahāyāna doctrine as taught by the Buddha, which consists of stripping the mind of all its attachments, not only to illusory externals but also to the very illusion of avoiding them, so as to accord with the absolute state wherein nothing can be grasped or rejected. This entails the eradication of space to reveal the all-embracing spiritual body, and time is simultaneously eliminated by the teaching of the non-existence of the past, the present and the future in order to expose the permanence of this essential body (Dharmakāya) which is beyond birth and death. When space and time vanish there remains nothing that can obstruct the self-nature of the practiser, who can thenceforth enjoy complete freedom and independence and who thereby reaches the stage of Full Enlightenment, that is Buddhahood.

The ancients had their unexcelled ways of teaching which seem strange to men of this modern age of materialism, not only in the West but also in the East. For the human mind is now more concerned with material than with spiritual values; it seeks only the satisfaction of its ever-increasing desires—though these are the very cause of our sufferings—and it casts away 'its own treasure house', which is its paradise of eternal bliss. So long as we allow our minds to discriminate and to grasp at illusions, the ancient teaching will seem strange, even stupid and silly, to us. However, if we succeed in disengaging our minds from externals—that is if we stop all our discriminating and discerning—the profundity of that teaching will become apparent to us, for it inculcates not only theory but also that practice which will give immediate results in the sphere of reality; for a teaching cannot be regarded as complete unless it gives the practical method of reaching the ultimate goal. When the Great Pearl preached his Dharma of Instantaneous Awakening, he taught its *doctrine*, its *aim*, its *substance* and its *function*; thus his teaching consists not only of the right interpretation and correct understanding of theory but also of the practical realization of *substance* and *function*, which are the two essentials of Complete Enlightenment. In other words, he taught the right Dharma which is immanent in every man and which does not come from outside.

The Master's numerous quotations from Mahāyāna sūtras, together with his unsurpassed interpretations and comments, show that all great Masters read the whole Tripiṭaka before or after their Enlightenment, and refute the unjustifiable contention that sūtras can be dispensed with in the Transmission of Mind introduced into China by the Twenty-Eighth Patriach Bodhidharma.

The Great Pearl urged his listeners not to let their minds abide anywhere and at the same time to keep from illusory non-abiding, so that a state of all-pervading purity and cleanness would appear of itself. And even this pure state should not be clung to, in order to release the mind from all remaining relativities and thereby attain realization of the 'patient endurance of the uncreate' (anutpattikadharma-kṣānti) which is an essential condition of Complete Enlightenment. Thus his instruction followed exactly the same pattern of the Dharma as laid down by the Buddha who said in the Sūtra of Complete Enlightenment that his disciples should keep themselves again and again from all illusions, including the illusory idea of keeping from them, so as to wipe out all traces of subject and object until nothing further remained to be avoided—for only then could Bodhi appear in full.

Therefore, Part One of this book gives the Mahāyāna instruction for self-realization of mind, for perception of self-nature and consequent attainment of Buddhahood. If we seriously follow this teaching and practise self-cultivation, beginning with the mind as the starting point, there is every possibility that we shall succeed in reaching the same mental states as those described by the Great Pearl in his twenty-eight-line gāthā.

Another wrong impression has been created in the West, owing to the false contention that the Buddha and the ancient Masters indulged in unnecessary repetitions when teaching their disciples. This point is ably explained in the Introduction by the author, who compares these repetitions to great hammer-blows intended to drive the adamantine nail well home, for the untrained human mind always refuses to be immobilized by self-control. Moroever, these so-called repetitions are in fact extremely necessary in order to give a true picture of the states of mind when passing through the various stages of meditation. For instance, when the Buddha said in the Diamond Sūtra: 'The past mind *cannot be found*, the present mind *cannot be found* and the future mind *cannot be found*', he actually described the three phases of meditation on the three *illusory* aspects of time, into which one cannot look simultaneously; for one has to enquire first into the past which has gone and is irrecoverable, then into the present which slips away as soon as one thinks of it, and then into the future which has not yet come.

Part Two of this book contains the dialogues between the Great Pearl and those who came to him for instruction. The Master's Dharma-words would sometimes seem strange and silly if they were translated literally without annotations. Even in China very few Buddhists of other schools understand the profound meaning hidden by such ordinary-seeming questions and answers. The author has apparently succeeded in taking the 'host' position when interpreting the text, and for the first time a British translator has presented the 'living meaning' of a Ch'an text. It is a matter for rejoicing that the deep meaning of the Ch'an School is being revealed in a book written by a Westerner, for up to now we have been accustomed to presentations of literal translations of Ch'an literature giving only its 'dead meaning'; this has been the chief cause of the misunderstanding of

Ch'an's Sublime Truth in the West. It is my fervent hope that more Western Buddhists will come forward to present authentic versions of the 'Transmission of the Mind', which is a short cut to spiritual awakening.

Hongkong   CHARLES LUK
(UPĀSAKA LU K'UAN YÜ)

TRANSLATOR'S INTRODUCTION

Invocation

Homage to my Teachers! Homage to the Three Precious Ones—the Buddha, Dharma and Sangha! Homage to That which Dwells Within Us All!

The Birth of this Translation

I have approached the task of rendering into English these teachings of the Zen Master Hui Hai, affectionately known as the Great Pearl, with more humility than when, years ago, I produced an incomplete translation of the same work. With the passing of years has come a deeper understanding of the inestimable worth of these teachings, together with a growing awareness of my own deficiencies both as a translator of words and as an interpreter of meanings. Though I do possess what for a Westerner is a fair knowledge of the kind of Chinese used in Buddhist works, as well as a long *acquaintance* with the Chinese forms of Mahāyāna Buddhism, these are but slender qualifications for the task. Ideally, the translator should be one who has penetrated so deeply into the subtle teachings of Ch'an (Zen) that he intuitively grasps the innermost meanings of the text. My only excuse for undertaking the work myself is that circumstances have made me peculiarly sensitive to the onward rush of 'Time's wingéd chariot'. Now that Buddhism is withering in China and being uprooted in Tibet, while the tawdry attractions of modern life continue to make dangerous inroads into the minds of the faithful in the remaining Buddhist countries, those who have even minimum qualifications must hasten if they are to preserve the essence of Buddhism for the West before most of the traditional links are broken or weakened beyond repair. There are already a good number of books on Buddhism in English, but many of them are by writers who, like myself, know only how to talk around and around it; so the most pressing need is for translations of original Sanskrit, Chinese, Tibetan and Japanese texts written by Masters, so called because, before setting brush to paper, they had already penetrated to Buddhism's heart. Such is my excuse and such the force which drove me to this short but very difficult task.

While passing the winter of 1959–60 in Kalimpong, a flower-girt townlet in the Himalayan foothills, I spent several hours a day seated at the feet of one or other of those saintly and learned monks who had recently fled their Tibetan monasteries in search of a haven where they could preach the Dharma without restraint or fear. Alas, my ignorance of Tibetan made me woefully dependent upon the services of that kind and patient Tibetan scholar and linguist, John Driver, who gave most generously of his time. Even so, I could not banish my sorrow at being so near and yet so cut off from monks with such precious knowledge to impart. Then, one day when I was gazing disconsolately at Kanchenjunga's majestic snowscape, the thought came to me that I was wasting valuable time in regrets as useless to myself as to others. Knowing nothing of Tibetan or Sanskrit, I did at least know something of Chinese Buddhist texts; my *Zen Teaching of Huang Po*, though far from being a masterpiece of translation, was even then affording some people an insight into the marvellous workings of an enlightened mind. So why not try again?

Thereupon, my thoughts flew back to a temple secluded in a long, low valley in West China where, during the Second World War, I had gone from my post at our embassy in Chungking to recuperate from illness. Today I do not even remember the temple's name, but I shall not easily forget what befell me there. It is strange (and no doubt a symptom of our need for books such as the Great Pearl's) how quickly the most delicious pleasures pall. Living in that peaceful temple, with nothing to do all day long beyond reading, sipping tea with friendly monks and gazing out at the beautiful pine-crowned ridges to either side of the fertile valley, I presently found myself bored! Beauty and idleness, to which years of hard work and a month of illness had made me look forward with all my heart, had all too quickly lost their charm. The aged monk-librarian, noticing with his shrewd old eyes my need for distraction, took me to spend a morning with him in the library—a large pavilion almost as big as the main shrine-hall of the temple. Inside I found most of it occupied not by books but by thousands of delicately incised boards of the kind formerly used for printing Chinese texts. Many of them were centuries old and bore vertical rows of characters so exquisitely formed that I was able to pass several happy hours handling and admiring them; but my state of health had left me weak and presently I felt the need to seek my bedroom, which opened off the shrine-hall on the other side of the courtyard. Just as I turned to go, the old monk smilingly placed in my hands a copy of one of the ancient texts block-printed from the boards I had been examining.

Back in my room, which even at midday was rather dark, I lighted a red votive candle and began idly glancing through the pages of the old gentleman's gift. It proved to be a reprint of an eighth-century (T'ang Dynasty) text composed by the Ch'an Master Hui Hai, together with a selection of his dialogues with his disciples. Almost at once I came upon an arresting quotation to the effect that sages seek from mind and not from the Buddha, whereas those who seek from the Buddha and not from mind are fools! This sharply awakened my curiosity, for it seemed extraordinary that a pious Buddhist writer should thus castigate those who seek something from the Teacher of Gods and Men. Anyone might be forgiven for finding such words blasphemous—as I did until I had read the whole book and begun to experience the first glimmer of understanding. There and then, I decided to try my hand at translating this intriguing work.

The first fruit of that decision was a little book entitled *The Way of Sudden Attainment*, containing a translation of the first half of our present text, which was kindly published by the Buddhist Society, London. I possess no copy of it now, but do not doubt that it was chock-full of errors due to the inexperience of the translator. I can only hope that I did not perpetrate too serious an injustice to the Great Pearl's wisdom; I am quite sure that much of the clarity of his exposition was lost. Now, some sixteen years later, I have translated the whole work, going back to the original text for my retranslation of the first part and translating the Tsung Ching Record for the first time.

The Method of Translation

In my present task I have been greatly assisted by three circumstances—a growing knowledge of Ch'an (Zen) Buddhism which, though still not at all profound, is better than it used to be; the notes on my first translation left me

by my old friend, the late I. T. Pun; and the invaluable
help given to me by Mr Charles Luk, who really is a profound Ch'an scholar. For this third and greatest piece of
good fortune I can find no words to express the fullness of
my gratitude and appreciation.

My rendering is, to a small extent, interpretive. That is
to say I have, in some cases, not hesitated to write into the
present text words which seemed to be implied in the force-
fully terse Chinese original; for a strictly literal translation
would be less intelligible than telegraphese. Moreover,
when a particular Chinese character has been employed
in various contexts I have not always rendered it by the
same word or phrase in English. Scholars may find this
blameworthy, but Chinese prose has something in common
with the poetry of all languages which makes it at once
full of depth and exceedingly difficult to translate—almost
every important word possesses so many shades of meaning
that the translator is compelled to select whichever shade
is most appropriate to the context and to omit or add
separately the meanings simultaneously implied. The am-
biguity of a word like 'hsin' (mind, heart, etc.) is admirable,
because in Buddhism not only are your mind, my mind,
his mind and uncreated, immortal MIND known to be one
in reality, but mind, minding and the thing minded (thought
about) are also held to be one and the same. The precision
of the English language, though so often a great advantage,
is in such cases as this a limiting factor which must detract
from the perfection of even the best possible translations.
A special list of terms difficult to translate adequately will
be found immediately before the Glossary.

Any reader who feels that here and there the style of the
text is more repetitious than suits his taste should, I think,
recollect that the Great Pearl in offering us precious Truth

B

is bestowing upon us the gift beyond all gifts—that of immortal wisdom and the peace which blossoms from it. Therefore he is at pains to make his words strike home; the repetitions are like great hammer-blows directed at the head of an adamantine nail that it may pierce and shine within the most secret places of the heart.

The numbers standing at the head of each subsection of the book are not to be found in the original; they have been inserted to indicate the paragraphing of the otherwise close-printed Chinese text and may be found useful for referring back to any particular part of the book.

The Universality of the Great Pearl's Teaching

I no longer possess a copy of the earlier translation I made of the first part of this work, but I seem to remember that in the Introduction, or perhaps in a note, I offered the opinion that Ch'an (Zen) has very little in common with Christian, Sufi or Hindu mysticism. If I really did write something like that I am sorry for it, for I have long since arrived at the conviction that the true mystics of all religions are Truth-Seers and that Ch'an (Zen) is of peculiar importance to the West for the very reason that it states in clear, god-free terms what Master Ekhart, St John of the Cross and their fellow-mystics experienced for themselves but saw fit to veil in the religious symbolism generally accepted by their contemporaries. Indeed, they had not much choice. Since the Ultimate Vision is a perception in which perceiver and perceiving are transcended and nothing remotely describable is perceived, the successful adept is left with three alternatives—to remain silent, thereby relinquishing all attempt to guide others towards the Goal; to clothe invisible Reality in the garments of the religion then and there prevailing; or to point the way by systematically demolishing all the categories of thought, such as colour, shape, size, existence, non-existence, space, time and so on. It is this last approach which gave rise to that school of Buddhism which, known in Sanskrit as Dhyāna and in Chinese as Ch'an or Ch'an-na, has reached the West under its Japanese name of Zen.

The Inevitable Complexity of Buddhism

When, some two and a half millenniums ago, the Lord Śākyamuni Buddha, also styled Gautama, preached the sublime doctrine whereby sentient beings can deliver themselves from Saṁsāra's endless round of birth, suffering, death and rebirth, he planted seeds which the winds of time carried as far afield from the Blessed One's native India as China, Mongolia, Tibet and Central Asia; Korea, Japan and Vietnam; Cambodia, Laos, Siam, Burma and Ceylon; besides many other countries since lost to Buddhism, such as Afghanistan, Malaya and Indonesia. Inevitably, seeds scattered across such widely differing soils have produced plants closely akin to one another in essentials but considerably different in appearance; and, naturally, the different climates, soils, waters, manures and methods of tending these plants have, over a period of much more than two thousand years, resulted in increasing these external differences. It happened that, quite early in Buddhist history, a division arose between the Mahāyānists and Theravādins (Hīnayānists) as to the correct interpretation of some of the Blessed One's teachings; and, since then, further subdivisions of those two main schools have, of course, arisen. As a result, Buddhism seems on the surface to be bewilderingly complex; strangers approaching it for the first time are puzzled by a vast number of sacred books in many languages which, as often as not, appear mutually contradictory; so it is not surprising that they—especially the scholars and logicians among them—shake their heads and sigh.

To employ a different simile, Buddhism is like a great walled city with so many gates that the stranger from a distant land despairs of finding his way to the citadel within. He fears to discover within the outer walls a complex maze of streets in which, not knowing the local customs and language, he may lose himself for ever—unable either to penetrate to the city's heart or to find his way back to one of the massive gateways. Yet, if he will boldly enter by any of those gates, he will find that the streets grow tolerably straight towards the centre and that all of them converge upon the one citadel.

The Basic Doctrine of Buddhism

In the above simile the citadel represents Buddhism's basic doctrine, which may be outlined in the following simple words: Life as we know it is, despite some pleasant, rainbow-hued facets, on the whole grim. Birth entails suffering for the mother and, presumably, for the child as well. Children are subject to mental woes which, although their causes often seem to us trifling, are as hard or even harder to bear than the genuine catastrophes awaiting them in later life. Grown men and women cannot help being aware that illness, bereavement or death may at any moment spring upon them, or that the incapacities of old age loom ahead; moreover, for countless numbers of people, the necessity for bitter toil and suffering caused by cold, hunger or near-starvation are almost always present; and even the most fortunate of men are truly remarkable if they can honestly say that their moments of happiness outnumber their combined moments of sorrow, grief, boredom and discontent. Many non-Buddhists take refuge in the idea of endless happiness to be enjoyed in a heavenly state to come; but, as all things in the universe which are observable by us are transient, and are not subject either to eternal existence or to cessation, but to endless transformations, it seems wiser to assume that what is not easily observable conforms to the same universal law of constant change. At any rate, Buddhists are convinced that we are likely to spend infinitely more than three score years and ten in these precarious surroundings, since birth and death succeed one another in endless procession, aeon upon aeon, for as long as we cling to the mistaken idea of our being separate, self-existent entities. Were there no way out of this dreadful cycle, sensitive and imaginative people might well recoil in horror or be driven to madness by the prospect of a fate infinitely more terrible than that of the Wandering Jew! Indeed, now that more and more people are turning away from the solace of religion, madness and severe neuroses are claiming a growing number of victims every year. The more 'progress' a people makes, the more 'civilized' a country becomes, the higher mounts the percentage of those requiring treatment for mental and neurotic diseases. Buddhism, however, does offer a hope of a relatively quick way out of the cycle of suffering. Castigated by the ignorant as a religion of pessimism, it actually fills its adherents with calm, smiling optimism.

The cause of all our sufferings and rebirths is—if we are compelled to state it rather inadequately in one word— desire, which, like many other Buddhist terms, is a word used to connote both itself and its own opposite, in this case aversion. It is because, in our ignorance, we cling to some things and abhor others that we have to revolve endlessly in Saṁsāra's round; for desire and aversion lead us to

think in such dualistic categories as self and other, existence and non-existence, good and bad, desirable and repulsive, and all the rest. We fail to see that this vast universe, with its beauty and its horror, is a creation of our
own minds—existing in that Mind with which our minds
are in truth identical. However, if we are willing to accept
this as at least a working hypothesis; if we begin training
ourselves to refrain from desire and aversion and from every
other kind of dualistic thought and behaviour; if we withdraw from the realm of appearances into the secret place
of the heart and surrender our so-called and previously
cherished 'selves' to its stillness, then mental creations will
gradually lose their power to afflict or disturb us. Whereat
our minds will become like polished mirrors, reflecting
every detail of the passing show and yet remaining unstained, perfectly unaltered by reflections of things, whether
beautiful or hideous. Gradually we shall achieve utter tranquillity; we shall cease responding to appearances with
outflows of will, passion, desire or aversion; when things
appear before us, we shall reflect them with our mirror-like
awareness; when they have passed by, they will leave no
stain and elicit from us not the smallest reaction. For a
mirror can reflect with the utmost clarity the exciting
loveliness of the naked bodies of Māra's lewd daughters or
the vile, passion-distorted faces of demons and yet remain
perfectly unmoved by lust or aversion; it makes no move
either to detain OR TO WITHDRAW FROM its objects; and
when these depart of their own accord it remains bright
and shining, unsullied, unpolluted by a single defiling
speck.

Buddhism teaches that it is the outflows resulting from
our varied responses to the play of phenomena which har-
ness us to Saṁsāra's round, to the Wheel of Life—the torture

wheel upon which the victim's bones are broken one by one and his flesh lacerated until, in his ignorance, he prays for the permanent death that is for ever denied him. Bound by our own folly and stupidity to this wheel, we are dragged upwards and downwards through the realms of life and death; every phenomenon produces a reaction within us, leading to some sort of outflow from our minds which acts upon phenomena and causes them to react upon us yet again—and so on, endlessly, until wisdom is painfully achieved. Until we have learnt to control our minds, every single thing perceived affects our consciousness or sub-consciousness exactly as a mirror would be affected if all the objects mirrored in it left their individual stains upon its surface! Whether that surface were stained by things 'good' or 'bad' would be immaterial, for their total con-glomeration would inevitably produce that dense, muddy colour we get from mixing all the paints in the paintbox in a single mess. Moreover, as every stain upon our minds caused by the objects of perception gives rise to outflows of lust, anger, greed, desire, aversion, love, hatred and so on, it sets up a chain-process of action, reaction, inter-reaction, which is endless. When, for the sake of convenience, Buddhists speak of desire as the cause of suffering, all that has been written here is implied in that single word—desire.

Critics have often asserted that Buddhism is a faith which preaches withdrawal from life, whereas in fact it teaches us neither to grasp at anything nor to withdraw from any-thing, but so to train ourselves that we may face everything with calm dispassion and without fear of stain. Moreover, it is our duty to exercise strenuous compassion directed at the welfare and release of all sentient beings—this cannot be accomplished by people who withdraw from difficulties.

As to the central Goal of Buddhism, it is this: When we have learnt (and in our turn taught) how to be utterly dispassionate, how to view all things in their essential oneness; when outflows cannot be enticed from us by any object whatsoever, nor the smallest stain be left upon our minds; then phenomena lose their power to defile and we dwell quiescently in the innate purity of our own minds, discovering moreover that these minds are not ours at all, but uncreated, everlasting MIND itself.

The Mahāyāna

When, during the last century, Western scholars were first attracted to Buddhism, various circumstances combined to bring them into intimate contact with Theravādin (Hīnayāna) sources at a time when very little was known to them of Mahāyāna. There were indeed some Russian scholars engaged in working upon Mahāyāna texts and in making contact with Mongolian and Tibetan monks, but their works were in Russian and not widely known outside their country. In their ignorance, the remaining Western scholars were too ready to accept the claim of the Theravādin monks of South-East Asia and Ceylon that they alone were the custodians of Buddhism 'in its pure form'. So Theravādin Buddhism was accepted in the West as 'orthodox' and the manifold methods employed by the Mahāyānists to achieve the common goal of Buddhism were looked upon askance. Western scholars used then to regard Mahāyāna as a hotchpotch of later developments leading away from the pristine purity of the Blessed One's teachings; so they attacked its doctrines with that fondness for narrow sectarianism which is a peculiar product of the West and directly contrary to the spirit of Buddhism; thereby arose a bias which has continued in some people's minds until today. It is as though Asian scholars, having made their first contact with Christianity in its Russian Orthodox form, were for ever afterwards to maintain that the Church of Rome and the Protestant Churches of the Further West are based upon mere heresies unworthy of study!

Nevertheless, quite apart from the fact that up-to-date research, coupled with closer contacts between Western scholars on the one hand and Chinese, Tibetan and Japanese monks on the other, has demonstrated how impossible it is to be sure that either Mahāyāna or Hīnayāna is the more 'orthodox' of the two, the folly of such narrowmindedness is clearly demonstrated by the Blessed One's own words; for, even according to the Theravādins, he seems to have declared roundly that whatsoever is conducive to the welfare of sentient beings is right doctrine and that whatsoever is harmful to their welfare cannot be true Buddha-Dharma. While it is true that some of the schools and sects within the Mahāyāna are of comparatively later origin than either the Theravādin or the ancient Mahāyānist sects, it is also true that they differ only as to method and never as to the Goal; therefore to argue that they are unorthodox is like arguing that almost every Christian community in the world is unorthodox because its members do not live, pray and perform their rites exactly in the manner of the contemporaries of St Peter or St Paul! When the Lord Buddha proclaimed that change and impermanence are inseparable from anything in this world, he did not suggest that the practice of Buddhism was to be (or could possibly be) an exception to this basic law. On the contrary, many of the sayings universally attributed to him indicate that he favoured changes of method to accord with differences of people, place and time; to him the

Goal—liberation from the round of birth and death for all
sentient creatures—was all-important; means to that end
he regarded as rafts to be constructed according to need,
used—and then cast away.

Varieties of Mahāyāna

For a number of reasons it befell that the more northerly
countries of the Buddhist world adopted the Mahāyāna
tradition, which is based on Sanskrit texts, whereas the
countries of South-East Asia adhered to the Theravādin
(Hīnayāna) tradition, based on Pali texts. Presently, within
the Mahāyāna itself, various schools and sects grew up and
flourished; yet they were not like sects in the Western sense
of that word, for there was seldom any mutual antipathy
and, until this day, it has often happened that members of
one sect have gladly sat at the feet of teachers belonging
to some other sect. Every Mahāyānist is free to adhere to
the sect into which he has, in a sense, been born or to join
any other sect which seems to him to be better adapted to
his powers or temperament. This happy condition is partly
due to Buddhist emphasis upon such qualities as compassion and mutual esteem, and partly to that spirit of
tolerance which, except under special circumstances, is a
normal characteristic of the peoples of the Further East.
In China, for example, I quite often discovered households
in which various members of the family were living amic-
ably together in spite of wide divergencies of religious faith
—the father being, perhaps, a Confucian; the mother a
Buddhist; and the daughter-in-law a Christian convert
from some missionary school or university. Moreover, in
some of the Chinese monasteries where I lived for a time,
there were often monks whose personal devotions, medita-
tions and studies were based on the teachings of the sect

of their choice, but who, nevertheless, joined whole-heartedly in whatever corporate services were required of them by the sect to which the monastery officially adhered. When I questioned them about this attitude, they were surprised by the suggestion of incongruity in their behaviour.

Another vital reason for the lack of disharmony among members of the various schools and sects of the Mahāyāna is that their mutual differences are mainly concerned with the emphasis given by each of them to one or more of the jointly accepted methods of achieving liberation. The Pure Land Sect stresses the spiritual condition (so highly prized by religious people everywhere) which is often called faith —an unshakable confidence in the existence and attain-ability of an Ultimate Perfection lying beyond the realm of ever-changing forms. The Vajrayāna School (Lamaism) emphasizes the underlying unity of Saṁsāra and Nirvāṇa, a fundamental but sometimes disregarded truth which in-dicates that liberation is not an escape from the one into the other, but a radical change of viewpoint resulting in recognition of their absolute identity, of the purely relative nature of their divergence. The Vajrayāna, like the Ch'an (Zen) School to which the Master Hui Hai belonged, is insistent that Nirvāṇa can be achieved (that is to say, rec-ognized or realized) here and now—IN THIS LIFE. The T'ien T'ai School (Japanese, Tendai) stresses the inter-relations between each single phenomenon and all others, interrelations so marvellous that the smallest part, when seen from above the space-time level, is found to contain the whole. The extinct Lü Tsung (Vinaya Sect) placed great emphasis upon the observance of about two hundred and fifty strict rules of conduct as a means of liberating the mind from the passions which obscure its purity. And so on.

The Emergence of the Dhyāna School

The last major division of the Mahāyāna arose in China some fifteen hundred years ago. It is called by the Chinese Ch'an or Ch'an-na and by the Japanese and most Westerners Zen—all three of these words being corruptions of the Sanskrit Dhyāna, which denotes the highest forms of the various Buddhist meditation and concentration practices, as well as the state of mind achieved by them. The doctrine of this school was introduced into (or, as many say, first preached in) China by the Indian missionary Bodhidharma, who is held to be the Twenty-Eighth Patriarch in direct line from Mahākāśyapa, to whom this doctrine was silently and intuitively transmitted by Śākyamuni Buddha himself. Bodhidharma came to China in the year A.D. 520 (or, as some now say, 420) and founded a line of patriarchs of whom the sixth and last was Hui Nêng, known in the West as Wei Lang, which is a corruption of the Cantonese Wei Nang. He was the propounder of the marvellous teachings contained in the *Sūtra of the Sixth Patriarch*, which has been translated into many languages, as it is a basic text for all Ch'an (Zen) Buddhists.

The Great Pearl or Ch'an Master Hui Hai

Although the patriarchate lapsed after Hui Nêng's death, the Dhyāna School, which we shall henceforth call Ch'an (Zen), continued to be very active and has remained so until today. Following Hui Nêng, numerous Masters arose, first in China and later in both China and Japan, whose teachings are still diligently read and applied. Among these Masters—the 'Early Fathers' of the Ch'an School—was one called Ma Tsu (died A.D. 788) whose monastery was in the province of Kiangsi. To him came devout students from all over the broad land of China, among them Hui Hai, the author of our text. Unfortunately, the nearest we can come to assigning the Master Hui Hai a date is to note that he was a disciple of Ma Tsu, who was presumably considerably the older of the two and who died on the fourth day of the second moon in the fourth year of Chen Yüan of the T'ang Dynasty, that is to say on the first of March A.D. 788.

Born in Yüeh Chou, which was probably the town now called Shao Hsing near Ning Po in the province of Chekiang, the Master Hui Hai had, prior to becoming a monk, the surname of Chu—a detail of special importance, as will soon be seen. At some time during his youth he entered the Great Cloud Monastery in his native city under the tutorship of the Venerable Tao Chih, who accordingly performed the ceremonial shaving of his head. Later, attracted no doubt by the great Ma Tsu's fame, he journeyed to Kiangsi and enrolled himself among that Master's disciples; and it was during a dialogue with Ma Tsu that he 'realized his mind', thus becoming enlightened. As will be seen from the Dialogues, he resided there six years and then returned to take care of the ageing Tao Chih, regarding this as his natural duty. Back in Yüeh Chou, he composed his famous Śāstra, the manuscript of which was carried off by another monk and shown to Ma Tsu. Ma Tsu was so impressed by it that he declared: 'In Yüeh Chou there is now a great pearl; its lustre penetrates everywhere freely and without obstruction.' That Hui Hai thenceforward became known as the Great Pearl was at once due to this richly deserved compliment and to his having formerly possessed in lay-life the surname of Chu; for this surname is identical in sound with the Chinese word for 'pearl', and the written forms of the two characters are very similar. Thereafter, the title stuck to him and, although Hui Hai (Ocean of Wisdom) was the religious name given him for life by his first teacher, he is generally referred to by the more picturesque title conferred on him by Ma Tsu.

Before remarking on the special qualities of the Great Pearl's Śāstra and the Dialogues which follow, it is necessary to say something of the teaching of the Ch'an (Zen) School in general.

The Purpose of Ch'an (Zen)

As will be seen from the Great Pearl's own words, he was an earnest exponent of the doctrine of Sudden Illumination which, at any rate from the time of the Sixth Patriarch onwards, has always been the central teaching of Ch'an; for this school came into prominence on a wave of reaction against the 'religiosity' by which, so its adherents felt, the force of Buddhism was being weakened. Apparently, many people had fallen into the belief that good works, piety, symbolical ceremonies and, above all, constant study and recitation of the sacred books could OF THEMSELVES advance the adept along the road to Enlightenment. Thus these people had lost sight of the Goal amid a welter of means; they had mistaken their rafts for the trees on the further shore. They no longer understood that good works, however admirable their immediate results, can only be of lasting benefit to the doer if he consciously applies the technique of relinquishment not only to money, time, energy and property, but also to the most cherished components of his own 'self' or personality. Nor did they remember that piety is of little use unless properly directed towards the eradication of the notion of a 'self', or that it is positively harmful to the pious one if it bolsters up that notion by affording him feelings of self-satisfaction, spiritual pride and so forth.

They forgot that symbolical ceremonies are meaningless unless properly used as a drill for stimulating those qualities which lead to the growth of wisdom and compassion, thereby eliminating all selfishness; and they did not see that the study of sacred books is a woeful waste of time unless the teachings contained in them are constantly applied by the adept to the uses he makes of his triple endowment of body, speech and mind.

The Central Doctrine of Ch'an (Zen)

The Ch'an Masters say in effect: 'Let us get to the root of things. Once we have heard, studied or intuitively discovered enough to know what Buddhism is about, let us relinquish everything in a tremendous effort to focus our minds on what is real. So long as our minds are out of focus, the objects of the senses, the sensations to which they give rise, and the stored results of those sensations, will impinge upon them, setting up endless chains of action and reaction. The process of correcting this wrong focus or false vision can be counted gradual only in the sense that most people require long and careful preparation; but true perception, when we have learnt how to be ready for it, will burst upon us in a flash. Though our minds remain out of focus by no more than, so to speak, a millionth of an inch, everything will still seem to us very nearly as it seemed before, despite our careful preparation; however, when true focus is attained, Reality will flash upon us, the whole universe of phenomena will be seen as it really is; its power to hamper and afflict us will be instantaneously destroyed, our remaining stores of karma will be burnt up in that flash, and nothing will remain for us except the duty of pointing the way so that others in their turn may achieve the Ultimate Vision just as we have done. When that final

intuition bursts upon us like a blinding light, we shall discover that nothing exists or ever has existed except in our
minds; that, indeed, our minds are not OUR minds but
MIND itself; that this Mind is perfectly quiescent, a pure
void in that it is utterly without form, characteristics,
opposites, plurality, subject, object or anything at all on
which to lay hold; and yet that it is certainly not void in
that it is the beginningless beginning and endless end of all
the phenomena which from moment to moment contribute
to the unceasing flux of what we call 'existence'. This void
is at once the container and the contained, the one and
the many, the neither-one-nor-many, the doomed and the
deathless, relativity and ultimate truth, Saṁsāra and Nirvāṇa, without a hairsbreadth of difference between any of
these or other pairs. Perceiving this, we shall seem to others
to have taken a sudden leap, as though from somewhere to
nowhere. Indeed, 'sudden leap', though inaccurate, is perhaps the best term with which to describe the process. Yet,
in truth, we shall have leapt from nowhere to nowhere;
hence, we shall not have leapt at all; nor will there be or
has there ever been any 'we' to make the leap! Nothing
will have changed except 'our' point of view. What was
formerly misperceived in the light of our little egos, 'we'
shall now rightly perceive in the glorious light of egoless-
ness. Thenceforward, though 'our' environment—the surrounding flux—will continue its moment-to-moment transformations as before, 'we' shall be capable of seeing all this
play of phenomena as tiny ripples upon the surface of
changelessness—'we' shall clearly recognize the changelessness of change! As a mirror impartially reflects green and
red, black and white, without being to the smallest extent
affected by any of them; as the spray of a waterfall reflects
all the colours of the rainbow without losing its colourless

purity; as dreamers behold acts of love and violence without moving so much as a hand; so does the mind of an Enlightened One react to the ceaseless play of phenomena. All of this will be more or less so in the deepest spiritual sense, and yet we should beware of taking these analogies of mirror, spray and dreamer too concretely, for even a mirror suggests a plurality of the reflector, the act of reflecting and the thing reflected, whereas these three do not in truth differ from one another; so that, beyond a certain point, even the mirror is a mere analogy—another raft to be discarded.

The Great Pearl's Śāstra and Dialogues

The general similarity of form found in the Śāstra itself and in the Dialogues which follow is due to the Great Pearl's preference, typical of the Ch'an (Zen) School as a whole, for the dialogue system of exposition. At the time when he wrote the former, he had not yet acquired any pupils, so it is clear that he composed the questions himself. Relieved of the necessity to provide the ornaments of style and verbal links which other forms of exposition require, he was able to achieve a forceful terseness which is very much to the point from beginning to end—a style which brings us closer to him, because he seems to be addressing us straight from his heart as though we were actually face to face with him. Yet, at the same time, his Śāstra possesses a great advantage over the books containing the teachings of many other Ch'an Masters, such as Huang Po, in that the Great Pearl composed it himself and could thus select and arrange his material as he wished, whereas what remains to us of the teachings of Huang Po and others consists only of what their disciples chose to record.

In a way, the present work is complementary to *The Zen Teaching of Huang Po*; for, while both Masters carry us to

C

the very heart of things, Huang Po deals rather more uniformly with the subject, whereas the Great Pearl relates each part of his exposition more specifically to some of the various tenets common to the Mahāyāna as a whole, or to particular tenets emphasized by this school or that, as well as to some of the doctrines of Taoism. It seems to me that Huang Po gives us a brilliant overall picture of the means of arriving at the Goal, and that the Great Pearl deals just as brilliantly but more precisely with most of the separate difficulties involved. For this reason, while his book is by no means of less interest than Huang Po's to the general reader, it will make a special appeal to those readers with a detailed knowledge of the various facets of traditional Buddhist doctrine.

There has been a tendency among some scholars, both Chinese and Western, to regard Ch'an (Zen) Buddhism as something much more apart from the general line of Mahāyāna Buddhist teaching and practice than the facts warrant. The present work should serve to correct that tendency, for it links branch and stem together in such a way as to make it obvious that the only real difference between them is one of emphasis. The Great Pearl's frequent references to the Mahāyāna Sūtras indicate that, though a staunch believer in the doctrine of sudden as opposed to gradual Illumination, he well understood the necessity of a thorough grounding in doctrine before the 'great leap' can be attempted. Indeed, the difference between the exponents of sudden and gradual Enlightenment is a more subtle one than at first appears; at times it may even be largely a verbal distinction; for, while imperfect perception (however slightly imperfect) cannot possibly be perception of the Absolute, of Reality itself, and we therefore remain in the dark right up to the final moment of

SUDDEN realization, yet that final moment must, with most beings, be the result of tremendous GRADUAL preparation. We can say that a drop of water boils suddenly, in that so long as its temperature remains even half a degree below boiling point it does not boil at all; or we may say that the boiling process is gradual in that it takes some time for the drop to reach the temperature at which it can boil. When the Master Hui Hai tells us that a sudden and perfect Illumination can take place within us in this very life, it is to be understood that this will happen only IF WE KNOW HOW TO ACCOMPLISH IT. The learning how is generally a gradual process, though it can be greatly shortened if, with the assistance of the Great Pearl's teaching, we learn just what to look for and how to set about it.

I do not think that the Great Pearl had any idea that we should realize our Buddha-Nature within a few minutes or days of digesting his Śāstra. His emphasis on suddenness has quite another meaning which may, perhaps, be imperfectly expressed as follows:

So long as we retain concepts of 'I' and 'other than I', of subject and object, of objective beings to be Enlightened, of their grasping at something objective called Enlightenment, of a 'thisness' and an 'otherness', we shall remain impossibly far from the Goal; in such cases, even millions of aeons spent in undertaking charitable works, in acquiring a theoretical knowledge of the sūtras and in other pious practices, will not help us to approach an inch nearer. Whereas, if we RELINQUISH EVERYTHING, including the notion of an 'I' to be Enlightened, as well as the notion of Enlightenment as something apart from or differing from anything else; if we understand that in reality there is no grasper, no grasping and no grasped; only then can we establish a point of view (at first theoretical) which will make us ripe for the sudden flash of Illumination that reveals the True Nature of ourselves and of everything else. Once this point of view is firmly established, and well tested by our gradually acquired ability to reflect (perceive) the infinitude of our surroundings with mirror-like stainlessness, we may hope to attain that sudden flash of Illumination very soon indeed—perhaps even in this life. There are, of course, formidable difficulties to be overcome, the last and very greatest of which is that, when Illumination is about to burst upon us, we may feel a sense of elation and accomplishment which will immediately throw us back to our starting point; for a sense of accomplishment implies an 'I' who accomplishes, an accomplishing and a something accomplished—wherefor, we shall hurtle back into the realm of duality, of pluralism, and all our efforts will have been in vain. Another great obstacle is that, while constantly reflecting on the voidness of opposites, on the unity of the Mind 'substance' common to all of us, we may grow attached to the concept of void, which will similarly throw us back upon the horns of duality—in that the concept of void is meaningless unless in opposition to the concept of non-void. Therefore, if we are to succeed, we must so train our minds as to free them absolutely from every concept whatsoever; there must be no thought either of attainment or of non-attainment, of void or of non-void; since monism is a rock no less precipitous than dualism. Furthermore, in training our minds towards that exalted, conceptless state, we must take ceaseless care to avoid becoming involved in likes and dislikes; we must learn to recognize all that is foul and horrible, all that is delicious and lovable, as being no more separate than ominous black rollers and the pure white crests of dancing wavelets are separate from the sea.

In order to free us from attachments to 'good', which

are apt to remain even when our attachments to 'evil' have
been overcome, the Great Pearl goes so far as to demolish
some of the basic tenets of Buddhism, just as rafts are
demolished or abandoned when they have served their
purpose so that carrying them further becomes an act of
stupidity. For example, Mahāyāna Buddhism teaches that
observance of the Six Pāramitās is essential to progress
along the Way—so, indeed, it is, up to an advanced point;
but, beyond that point, even consciously virtuous conduct
must be relinquished along with everything else. The śīlapāramitā (observing the precepts), the kṣāntipāramitā
(perfect forbearance), the vīryapāramitā (firm zealous-
ness), the dhyānapāramitā (meditative concentration leading to one-pointedness of mind) and the prajñāpāramitā
(wisdom) must all be swallowed up in the dānapāramitā
(relinquishment) in the sense that even the pāramitās
themselves must presently be relinquished lest, by clinging
to them, we permit a distinction between one kind of behaviour and another to occupy our minds. (Naturally, these
pāramitās must never be relinquished until we have reached
the stage where total relinquishment becomes possible; to
relinquish them before we have subdued our passions and
lusts would be the very reverse of Buddhist conduct.)

Another tenet universally accepted within the Mahāyāna
is that progress along the Bodhisattva's Way requires the
simultaneous practice of śīla (morality and discipline),
dhyāna (meditation, concentration and all the various
mental exercises designated by these insufficient English
terms) and prajñā (wisdom and learning). These, also, are
entirely necessary up to a point; beyond it, they must be
relinquished with the rest. Similarly, the Trikāya doctrine
has ultimately to be relinquished. According to this doctrine, the Buddhas (and therefore all sentient beings, who

are equally Buddhas except that they have yet to realize their Buddha-Nature) possess three Bodies—the Dharma-kāya in which they rest indivisible from the Absolute, the Sambhogakāya in which they enjoy the rewards of having freed themselves from worldly ties and in which they can appear to other beings in insubstantial form, and the Nir-māṇakāya in which they take on physical characteristics similar to those of ordinary men. Moreover, the Dharma-kāya, as will be seen from the Śāstra, is occasionally con-ceived of as having five separate aspects. However real these distinctions may be in relation to the plane of mani-fold phenomena, ultimately there cannot be the smallest difference between them, in that everything within and without the phenomenal sphere shares a single 'substance' or True Nature with everything else. So it is with the Triloka or Three Worlds—the kāmadhātu (worlds like ours in which sensuous desire for sex, food and so on plays its part), the rūpadhātu (worlds or heavens in which forms of beings and objects are distinguishable rather like those in the calmer sorts of dream, but wherein sensuous desire is not to be found) and the arūpadhātu (formless realms of pure spirit or pure contemplation); ultimately, we must re-linquish this and every other doctrine suggestive of dualism or pluralism. Yet, having done so, we must beware of taking the Mahāyāna doctrine that everything is śūnya (void) to imply a mere nothingness or total cessation of everything, for Śūnyatā (the Absolute conceived of as perfect voidness) is identical with the Garbhadhātu (the Absolute conceived of as the womb of all phenomena).

What remains when all distinctions are seen as void, and when void itself is voided, is the inexpressible mystery awaiting the time of our Illumination. The Great Pearl does not attempt to describe it, since the task would be futile. When we have perfectly followed out his directions by eschewing love, aversion and all the rest, by rejecting all concepts which can possibly land us upon the horns of dualism, by striving with might and main until even striving itself can be relinquished together with the very notion of a striver or something to strive for, we shall no doubt discover that inexpressible mystery for ourselves. Meanwhile, his repeated advice to us is to strive and strive and strive, but never for one moment with a notion of anything objective to be attained. Those mystics who, unlike the Great Pearl, have tried to clothe the Ultimate in words have often succeeded in adding to the obscurations hiding it from our view.

The Technique of Dhyāna-Practice

An important technique aiming at that perfect mind-control by which the achievementless achievement is achieved is that of dhyāna (here meaning ch'an-ting or zazen), whereby the mind is turned inward upon itself and the innermost recesses of our being are so well explored that we at last come face to face with that unsullied Mind which is neither yours nor mine, nor anybody else's, and yet discoverable in all of us. Readers of books such as this will naturally feel disappointed when they discover few detailed instructions for the performance of this difficult technique, but it was the practice of the Ch'an Masters to communicate these instructions verbally. The technique is difficult to explain—there are no satisfactory words for it and the advice required will depend upon the personality and so on of each student. Just for these reasons, it used to be imparted to pupils living under a Master's direct supervision. However, now that Ch'an (Zen) is becoming popular in the West, the oft-found injunction not to practise without a Teacher is found impossible to observe because, while qualified adepts are hard to encounter even in Asia, in other continents they are infinitely rare. So we must do the best we can by carefully studying the original works of the great Zen Masters, such as the Great Pearl, and by seeking to interpret them intuitively.

Besides building a firm foundation by careful reading, preliminary Zen practice involves all of the following—constant attention, whether 'walking, standing, sitting or lying', to the play of phenomena around us and within us; an unremitting effort to see this play in the light of the truths we are learning; a gradual reduction of our outflows by recognizing mental and physical phenomena for the illusions they are and therefore refusing to be stained by them; the cultivation of mirror-like reactions instead of reacting with minds like sensitive (i.e. easily stained) spools of film; the exercise of ever-widening compassion to all living beings; and at least the simpler kinds of formal meditation. For this last, the aspirant should choose a clean, quiet place and, if he lives in a noisy city, the quietest hours of the very early morning, or of the night. Ideally, he should be able to sit upright with legs folded upon a floor-cushion, but an upright, NON-RIGID position in a chair may suit those too old to learn how to sit comfortably with their legs crossed in the usual Buddhist way. Techniques requiring long hours of strenuous meditation and all but the simplest breathing exercises are EXCEEDINGLY DANGEROUS without the guidance of an expert Teacher.

Our not being able to venture immediately beyond preliminary practice is no cause for despair. Even those Chinese, Japanese, Tibetan and Mongol adepts who tread the Short Path fully determined to reach Illumination in this life never dream of dispensing with several years of constant night-and-day preliminary study and practice.

Moreover, if we practise Ch'an (Zen), it must surely be because we accept its cardinal doctrines; and, if we do accept them, we come to realize that this present life-period of ours is but a single moment in eternity, a single link in a chain stretching back to beginningless time, which will, unless we burst it asunder, stretch forward for aeon upon aeon to come. Having acquired this right perspective, we need not be over-impatient, especially as we can be sure that preliminary practice carried out zealously during this life-period will, *in case we do not attain full success here and now*, so ripen us that we shall be born with opportunities for going deeper and achieving liberation in the very next life. Nor must it be forgotten that some people are so conditioned by their previous lives that they will be able to advance much more quickly than they expect, and perhaps attain liberation in this life, as did the Great Pearl himself. We must be careful, though, not to deceive ourselves. Our fellow-adepts sometimes prove all too willing to suppose that we have advanced much further than we have, we must not let their admiration convince us that it is deserved. Besides, we ourselves may so easily mistake the minor forms of bliss which sometimes arise quite early in our practice for true Illumination, especially as, mind's 'substance' being one, they are related to it. When true Illumination comes, we can no more doubt it than a diver doubts he has plunged into the water. For Illumined people, the whole universe is permanently transformed! Until that happens, we must faithfully follow the Great Pearl's advice —'Strive on! Strive on!'

MAY ALL BEINGS ATTAIN RELEASE!

JOHN BLOFELD

The Bamboo Studio

PART ONE

THE ZEN TEACHING OF HUI HAI
on Sudden Illumination

Being a translation of Ch'an Master Hui Hai's own Śāstra, the Tun Wu Ju Tao Yao Mên Lun *or* A Treatise on the Essential Gateway to Truth by Means of Instantaneous Awakening.

1. Humbly I prostrate myself before the Buddhas of the Ten Quarters[1] and the Excellent Company of Bodhisattvas. In setting forth this treatise, I am apprehensive that I may fail correctly to interpret the Sacred Mind. If so, may I be given a chance for repentance and reform. However, if I do succeed in imparting the Sacred Truth, I dedicate the resultant merit to all living beings in the hope that each of them will attain Buddhahood in his next life.

*   *   *

2. Q: What method must we practise in order to attain deliverance?[2]

A: It can be attained only through a sudden Illumination.[3]

Q: What is a sudden Illumination?

A: Sudden means ridding yourselves of deluded thoughts[4] instantaneously. Illumination means the realization that Illumination is not something to be attained.

Q: From where do we start this practice?

A: You must start from the very root.

Q: And what is that?

A: MIND is the root.

Q: How can this be known?

A: The Laṅkāvatāra Sūtra says: 'When mental processes (hsin) arise, then do all dharmas (phenomena) spring forth; and when mental processes cease, then do all dharmas cease likewise.' The Vimalakīrti Sūtra says: 'Those desiring to attain the Pure Land[5] must first purify their own minds, for the purification of mind IS the purity of the Buddha-Land.' The Sūtra of the Doctrine Bequeathed by the Buddha says: 'Just by mind-control, all things become possible to us.' In another sūtra it says: 'Sages seek from mind, not from the Buddha; fools seek from the Buddha instead of seeking from mind. Wise men regulate their minds rather than their persons; fools regulate their persons rather than their minds.' The Sūtra of the Names of the Buddha states: 'Evil springs forth from the mind, and by the mind is evil overcome.' Thus we may know that all good and evil proceed from our minds and that mind is therefore the root. If you desire deliverance, you must first know all about the root. Unless you can penetrate to this truth, all your efforts will be vain; for, while you are still seeking something from forms external to yourselves, you will never attain. The Dhyānapāramitā Sūtra says: 'For as long as you direct your search to the forms around you, you will not attain your goal even after aeon upon aeon; whereas, by contemplating your inner awareness, you can achieve Buddhahood in a single flash of thought.'

Q: By what means is the root-practice to be performed?

A: Only by sitting in meditation, for it is accomplished by dhyāna (ch'an) and samādhi (ting). The Dhyāna-

pāramitā Sūtra says: 'Dhyāna and samādhi are essential
to the search for the sacred knowledge of the Buddhas; for,
without these, the thoughts remain in tumult and the roots
of goodness suffer damage.'

Q: Please describe dhyāna and samādhi.

A: When wrong thinking ceases, that is dhyāna; when
you sit contemplating your original nature,[6] that is samādhi,
for indeed that original nature is your eternal mind. By
samādhi, you withdraw your minds from their surroundings, thereby making them impervious to the eight winds,
that is to say, impervious to gain and loss, calumny and
eulogy, praise and blame, sorrow and joy. By concentrating
in this way, even ordinary people may enter the state of
Buddhahood. How can that be so? The Sūtra of the Bod-
hisattva-Precepts says: 'All beings who observe the Buddha-
Precept thereby enter Buddhahood.' Other names for this
are deliverance, gaining the further shore, transcending the
six states of mortal being,[7] o'erleaping the three worlds,[8]
or becoming a mighty Bodhisattva, an omnipotent Sage, a
Conqueror!

*   *   *

3. Q: Whereon should the mind settle and dwell?

A: It should settle upon non-dwelling and there dwell.

Q: What is this non-dwelling?

A: It means not allowing the mind to dwell upon anything whatsoever.

Q: And what is the meaning of that?

A: Dwelling upon nothing means that the mind is not
fixed upon good or evil, being or non-being, inside or outside or somewhere between the two, void or non-void, concentration or distraction. This dwelling upon nothing is the

state in which it should dwell; those who attain to it are said to have non-dwelling minds—in other words, they have Buddha-Minds!

Q: What does mind resemble?

A: Mind has no colour, such as green or yellow, red or white; it is not long or short; it does not vanish or appear; it is free from purity and impurity alike; and its duration is eternal. It is utter stillness. Such, then, is the form and shape of our original mind, which is also our original body —the Buddhakāya![9]

Q: By what means do this body or mind perceive? Can they perceive with the eyes, ears, nose, sense of touch and consciousness?

A: No, there are not several means of perception like that.

Q: Then, what sort of perception is involved, since it is unlike any of those already mentioned?

A: It is perception by means of your own nature (svabhāva). How so? Because your own nature being essentially pure and utterly still, its immaterial and motionless 'substance' is capable of this perception.[10]

Q: Yet, since that pure 'substance' cannot be found, where does such perception come from?

A: We may liken it to a bright mirror which, though it contains no forms, can nevertheless 'perceive' all forms. Why? Just because it is free from mental activity. If you students of the Way had minds unstained,[11] they would not give rise to falsehood and their attachment to the subjective ego and to objective externals would vanish; then purity would arise of itself and you would thereby be capable of such perception. The Dharmapāda Sūtra says: 'To establish ourselves amid perfect voidness in a single flash is excellent wisdom indeed!'

*   *   *

4. Q: According to the Vajra-Body Chapter of the Mahā-parinirvāṇa Sūtra, 'the (indestructible) diamond-body[12] is imperceptible, yet it clearly perceives; it is free from dis-cerning and yet there is nothing which it does not compre-hend'. What does this mean?

A: It is imperceptible because its own nature is a form-less 'substance' which is intangible; hence it is called im-perceptible; and, since it is intangible, this 'substance' is observed to be profoundly still and neither vanishing nor appearing. Though not apart from our world, it cannot be influenced by the worldly stream; it is self-possessed and sovereign, which is the reason why it clearly perceives. It is free from discerning in that its own nature is formless and basically undifferentiated. Its comprehending everything means that the undifferentiated 'substance' is endowed with functions as countless as the sands of the Ganges; and, if all phenomena were to be discerned simultaneously, it would comprehend all of them without exception. In the Prajñā Gāthā it is written:

> Prajñā, unknowing, knoweth all;
> Prajñā, unseeing, seeth all.

*   *   *

5. Q: There is a sūtra which says that not to perceive anything in terms of being or non-being is true deliverance. What does it mean?

A: When we attain to purity of mind, that is something which can be said to exist. When this happens, our remain-ing free from any thought of achievement is called not per-ceiving anything as existent; while reaching the state in which no thoughts arise or persist, yet without being con-scious of their absence, is called not perceiving anything as non-existent. So it is written: 'Not to perceive anything in terms of being and non-being', etc. The Śūraṅgama Sūtra says: 'Perceptions employed as a base for building up positive concepts are the origin of all ignorance (avidyā);[13] perception that there is nothing to perceive—that is Nir-vāṇa, also known as deliverance.'

*   *   *

6. Q: What is the meaning of 'nothing to perceive'?

A: Being able to behold men, women and all the various sorts of appearances while remaining as free from love or aversion as if they were actually not seen at all—that is what is meant by 'nothing to perceive'.

Q: That which occurs when we are confronted by all sorts of shapes and forms is called perception. Can we speak of perception taking place when nothing confronts us?

A: Yes.

Q: When something confronts us, it follows that we perceive it, but how can there be perception when we are confronted by nothing at all?

A: We are now talking of that perception which is independent of there being an object or not. How can that be? The nature of perception being eternal, we go on perceiving whether objects are present or not.[14] Thereby we come to understand that, whereas objects naturally appear and disappear, the nature of perception does neither of those things; and it is the same with all your other senses.

Q: When we are looking at something, does the thing looked at exist objectively within the sphere of perception or not?

A: No, it does not.

Q: When we (look around and) do not see anything, is there an absence of something objective within the sphere of perception?

A: No, there is not.

*   *   *

7. Q: When there are sounds, hearing occurs. When there are no sounds, does hearing persist or not?

A: It does.

Q: When there are sounds, it follows that we hear them, but how can hearing take place during the absence of sound?

A: We are now talking of that hearing which is independent of there being any sound or not. How can that be? The nature of hearing being eternal, we continue to hear whether sounds are present or not.

Q: If that is so, who or what is the hearer?

A: It is your own nature which hears and it is the inner cognizer who knows.[15]

Q: As to the gateway of sudden Illumination, what are its doctrine, its aim, its substance and its function?[16]

A: To refrain from thinking (nien) is its doctrine; not to allow wrong thoughts to arise is its aim; purity is its substance and wisdom is its function.

Q: We have said that its doctrine is to refrain from thinking, but we have not yet examined the meaning of this term. What is it that we must refrain from thinking about?

A: It means that we must refrain from wrong thinking, but not from right thinking.

Q: What are wrong thinking and right thinking?

A: Thinking in terms of being and non-being is called wrong thinking, while not thinking in those terms is called

D

right thinking. Similarly, thinking in terms of good and evil is wrong; not to think so is right thinking. The same applies to all the other categories of opposites—sorrow and joy, beginning and end, acceptance and rejection, dislikes and likes, aversion and love, all of which are called wrong thinking, while to abstain from thinking in those categories is called right thinking.

Q: Please define right thinking (more positively).

A: It means thinking solely of Bodhi (Enlightenment).

Q: Is Bodhi something tangible?

A: It is not.

Q: But how can we think solely of Bodhi if it is intangible?

A: It is as though Bodhi were a mere name applied to something which, in fact, is intangible, something which never has been nor ever will be attained. Being intangible, it cannot be thought about, and it is just this not thinking about it which is called rightly thinking of Bodhi as something not to be thought about—for this implies that your mind dwells upon nothing whatsoever. The term 'not to be thought about' is like the various kinds of not-thinking mentioned earlier, all of which are but names convenient for use in certain circumstances—all are of the one substance in which no differences or diversities exist. Simply to be conscious of mind as resting upon nothing whatsoever is to be without thought; and whoever reaches this state is naturally delivered.

*   *   *

8. Q: What is the meaning of to act as the Buddhas do?

A: It means total abstention from action,[17] which is also termed right or holy action. It is very similar to what we were talking about before, for it means not acting as if things really are or are not, and not acting from motives of aversion, love and all the rest. The Great Canon of Monastic Rules says: 'The Sages do not act like other beings; nor do other beings act like the Sages.'

*   *   *

9. Q: What does right perception mean?

A: It means perceiving that there is nothing to perceive.

Q: And what does that mean?

A: It means beholding all sorts of forms, but without being stained by them as no thoughts of love or aversion arise in the mind. Reaching this state is called obtaining the Buddha-Eye, which really means just that and nothing else. Whereas, if the spectacle of various forms produces love or aversion in you, that is called perceiving them as though they had objective existence, which implies having the eye of an ordinary person, for indeed ordinary people have no other sort of eye. It is the same with all the other organs of perception.

*   *   *

10. Q: When you said that wisdom is the function, what did you mean by wisdom?

A: The knowledge that by realizing the voidness of all opposites deliverance is assured and that, without this realization, you will never gain deliverance. This is what we call wisdom or knowing wrong from right. Another name for it is knowing the function of the 'substance'. Concerning the unreality of opposites, it is the wisdom inherent in the 'substance' which makes it known that to realize their voidness means liberation and that there can be no more doubt about it. This is what we mean by function. In speaking thus of the unreality of opposites, we refer to the non-existence of relativities such as 'is' and 'is not', good and evil, love and aversion, and so on.

Q: By what means can the gateway of our school be entered?

A: By means of the dānapāramitā.

Q: According to the Buddha, the Bodhisattva-Path comprises six pāramitās. Why, then, have you mentioned only the one? Please explain why this one alone provides a sufficient means for us to enter.

A: Deluded people fail to understand that the other five all proceed from the dānapāramitā and that by its practice all the others are fulfilled.

Q: Why is it called the dānapāramitā?

A: Dāna means relinquishment.

Q: Relinquishment of what?

A: Relinquishment of the dualism of opposites.

Q: Which means?

A: It means total relinquishment of ideas as to the dual nature of good and bad, being and non-being, love and aversion, void and non-void, concentration and distraction, pure and impure. By giving all of them up, we attain to a state in which all opposites are seen as void. The real practice of the dānapāramitā entails achieving this state without any thought of 'Now I see that opposites are void' or 'Now I have relinquished all of them'. We may also call it the simultaneous cutting off of the myriad types of concurrent causes; for it is when these are cut off that the whole Dharma-Nature becomes void; and this voidness of the Dharma-Nature means the non-dwelling of the mind upon anything whatsoever. Once that state is achieved, not a single form can be discerned. Why? Because our self-nature is immaterial and does not contain a single thing (foreign to itself). That which contains no single thing is true Reality, the marvellous form of the Tathāgata. It is said in the Diamond Sūtra: 'Those who relinquish all forms are called Buddhas (Enlightened Ones).'

Q: However, the Buddha did speak of six pāramitās, so why do you now say they can all be fulfilled in that one? Please give your reason for this.

A: The Sūtra of the Questions of Brahma says: 'Jāla-vidyā, the Elder, spoke unto Brahma and said: "Bodhi-sattvas by relinquishing all defilements (kleśa) may be said to have fulfilled the dānapāramitā, also known as total relinquishment; being beguiled by nothing, they may be said to have fulfilled the śīlapāramitā, also known as observing the precepts; being hurt by nothing, they may be said to have fulfilled the kṣāntipāramitā, also known as exercising forbearance; clinging to nothing, they may be said to have fulfilled the vīryapāramitā, also known as exercising zeal; dwelling on nothing, they may be said to have fulfilled the dhyānapāramitā, also known as practising dhyāna and samādhi; speaking lightly of nothing, they may be said to have fulfilled the prajñāpāramitā, also known as exercising wisdom. Together, they are named the six methods." ' Now I am going to speak about those six methods in a way which means precisely the same—the first entails relinquishment; the second, no arising (of perception, sensation, etc., etc., etc.); the third, no thinking; the fourth, remaining apart from forms; the fifth, non-abiding (of the mind); and the sixth, no indulgence in light speech. We give different names to these six methods only for convenience in dealing with passing needs; for, when we come to the marvellous principle involved in them all,

we find no differences at all. So you have only to understand that, by a single act of relinquishment, EVERYTHING
is relinquished; and that no arising means no arising of
anything whatsoever. Those who have lost their way have
no intuitive understanding of this; that is why they speak
of the methods as though they differed from one another.
Fools bogged down in a multiplicity of methods revolve
endlessly from life-span to life-span. I exhort you students
to practise the way of relinquishment and nothing else, for
it brings to perfection not only the other five pāramitās
but also myriads of dharmas (methods).

*   *   *

11. Q: What are the 'three methods of training (to be
performed) at the same level' and what is meant by performing them on the same level?

A: They are discipline (vinaya), concentration (dhyāna)
and wisdom (prajñā).[18]

Q: Please explain them one by one.

A: Discipline involves stainless purity.[19] Concentration
involves the stilling of your minds so that you remain
wholly unmoved by surrounding phenomena. Wisdom
means that your stillness of mind is not disturbed by your
giving any thought to that stillness, that your purity is un-
marred by your entertaining any thought of purity and
that, in the midst of all such pairs of opposites as good and
evil, you are able to distinguish between them without
being stained by them and, in this way, to reach the state
of being perfectly at ease and free of all dependence. Furthermore, if you realize that discipline, concentration and
wisdom are all alike in that their substance is intangible
and that, hence, they are undivided and therefore one—

that is what is meant by three methods of training performed at the same level.

*   *   *

12. Q: When the mind rests in a state of purity, will that
not give rise to some attachment to purity?

A: If, on reaching the state of purity, you refrain from
thinking 'now my mind is resting in purity', there will be
no such attachment.

Q: When the mind rests in a state of void, will that not
entail some attachment to void?

A: If you think of your mind as resting in a state of
void, then there will be such an attachment.

Q: When the mind reaches the state of not dwelling
upon anything, and continues in that state, will there
not be some attachment to its not dwelling upon
anything?

A: So long as your mind is fixed solely on void, there is
nothing to which you can attach yourself. If you want to
understand the non-dwelling mind very clearly, while you
are actually sitting in meditation, you must be cognizant
only of the mind and not permit yourself to make judgements—that is, you must avoid evaluations in terms of
good, evil or anything else. Whatever is past is past, so do
not sit in judgement upon it; for, when minding about the
past ceases of itself, it can be said that there is no longer any
past. Whatever is in the future is not here yet, so do not
direct your hopes and longings towards it; for, when
minding about the future ceases of itself, it can be said that
there is no future.[20] Whatever is present is now at hand;
just be conscious of your non-attachment to everything—
non-attachment in the sense of not allowing any love or

aversion for anything to enter your mind; for, when minding the present ceases of itself, we may say that there is no
present. When there is no clinging to any of those three
periods, they may be said not to exist.

Should your mind wander away, do not follow it, whereupon your wandering mind will stop wandering of its own
accord. Should your mind desire to linger somewhere, do
not follow it and do not dwell there, whereupon your mind's
questing for a dwelling-place will cease of its own accord.
Thereby, you will come to possess a non-dwelling mind—
a mind which remains in the state of non-dwelling. If you
are fully aware in yourself of a non-dwelling mind, you
will discover that there is just the fact of dwelling, with
nothing to dwell upon or not to dwell upon. This full
awareness in yourself of a mind dwelling upon nothing is
known as having a clear perception of your own mind or,
in other words, as having a clear perception of your own
nature. A mind which dwells upon nothing is the Buddha-
Mind, the mind of one already delivered, Bodhi-Mind,
Uncreate Mind; it is also called realization that the nature
of all appearances is unreal. It is this which the sūtras call
'patient realisation of the Uncreate'.[21] If you have not
realized it yet, you must strive and strive, you must in-
crease your exertions. Then, when your efforts are crowned
with success, you will have attained to understanding from
within yourself—an understanding stemming from a mind
that abides nowhere, by which we mean a mind free from
delusion and reality alike. A mind disturbed by love and
aversion is deluded; a mind free from both of them is real;
and a mind thus freed reaches the state in which opposites
are seen as void, whereby freedom and deliverance are
obtained.

*   *   *

13. Q: Are we to make this effort only when we are sitting in meditation, or also when we are walking about?

A: When I spoke just now of making an effort, I did not mean only when you are sitting in meditation; for, whether you are walking, standing, sitting, lying or whatever you are doing, you must uninterruptedly exert yourselves all the time. This is what we call constantly abiding (in that state).

14. Q: The Vaipula Sūtra says 'Of the five kinds of Dharmakāya,[22] the first is the Dharmakāya of the Absolute; the second is the Dharmakāya of Merit; the third is the Dharmakāya of the Dharma-Nature;[23] the fourth is the Dharmakāya of Infinite Manifestations; and the fifth is the Dharmakāya of the Void.' Which one is our own body?

A: To comprehend that mind is imperishable is to possess the Dharmakāya of the Dharma-Nature. To comprehend that all the myriad forms are contained in mind is to possess the Dharmakāya of Merit. To comprehend that mind is not mind is to possess the Dharmakāya of the True Nature of All. To teach living beings according to their individual capacities for conversion is to possess the Dharmakāya of Infinite Manifestation. To comprehend that mind is formless and intangible is to possess the Dharmakāya of the Void. If you understand the meaning of all this, it implies that you know there is nothing to be achieved. Realizing that there is nothing tangible, nothing achievable —this is achieving the Dharmakāya of the Buddha-Dharma.[24] Anyone who supposes he can achieve it by getting hold of or grasping at something is full of self-conceit—an arrogant fellow[25] with perverted views, a man of heterodox beliefs. The Vimalakīrti Nirdeśa Sūtra says: 'Śāriputra enquired of a devakanyā:[26] "What is it you have won? What achievement has given you such powers of speech?" To which the devakanyā replied: "It was my winning and achieving nothing which enabled me to reach this state. According to the Buddha-Dharma, someone who wins and achieves things is a person full of self-conceit." '

*   *   *

15. Q: The sūtras speak not only of Samyak-Sambodhi[27] (Full Enlightenment), but also of a Marvellous Enlightenment[28] lying even beyond that. Please explain these terms.

A: Samyak-Sambodhi is the realization of the identity of form and voidness. Marvellous Enlightenment is the realization of the absence of opposites, or we can say that it means the state of neither Enlightenment nor non-Enlightenment.

Q: Do these two sorts of Enlightenment really differ or not?

A: Their names are expediently used for the sake of temporary convenience, but in substance they are one, being neither dual nor different. This oneness and sameness characterize ALL phenomena of whatever kind.

*   *   *

16. Q: What is the meaning of a passage in the Diamond Sūtra which states that 'having absolutely nothing describable in words is called preaching the Dharma'?

A: Prajñā (wisdom) is a substance of absolute purity which contains no single thing on which to lay hold. This is the meaning of 'nothing describable in words'. Yet that immaterial and motionless Prajñā is capable of whatever functions are befitting—functions as numerous as the sands of the Ganges; so there is nothing at all which it does not comprehend; and this is what is implied by the words 'preaching the Dharma'. Therefore is it written: 'Having absolutely nothing describable in words is called preaching the Dharma.'

Q: (The Diamond Sūtra also says) 'If a virtuous man or woman holds to, studies and recites this sūtra, and is despised by others, this person, who was bound to suffer an evil destiny in retribution for his past sins and whose karmic sins are now eradicated by the others' contempt, will attain Anuttara-Samyak-Saṁbodhi.' Please explain this.

A: Their case resembles that of a man who, not having met an enlightened Teacher, continues building up nothing but evil karma for himself, so that his pure original mind, obscured by the three poisons[29] stemming from primordial ignorance, cannot show forth, which is the reason for our calling him despicable. Then, just because he is despised in this life, he grows determined to seek out the Way of the Buddhas without delay; and, thereby, his ignorance is conquered so that the three poisons cease to be generated, whereat his original mind shines forth brilliantly. The tumult of his thoughts is thenceforth stilled, for all the evil in him has been destroyed. It is his having been despicable which has led to the conquest of ignorance, the cessation of his mental tumult and—as a natural consequence of that —to his deliverance. Therefore is it written that Bodhi is attainable at the very moment we make up our minds to achieve it—that is to say IN THIS LIFE and not in some other lives to come.

Q: It is also written that the Tathāgata has five kinds of Vision. What are they?

A: The perception that all appearances are pure (i.e.

real) is called Earthly Vision. The perception that their substance is pure (real) is called Heavenly Vision. Ability to distinguish the minutest differences among the appearances constituting our environment, as well as the smallest gradations of good and evil, and yet to be so entirely unaffected by them that we remain perfectly at ease amidst all of them[30]—that is called the Wisdom Vision. The perception that there is nothing to perceive is called the Dharma Vision. No perception, yet nothing unperceived, is called the Buddha Vision.

Q: It is also written that there is a Great Vehicle (Mahāyāna) and a Supreme Vehicle. What are they?

A: The former is that of the Bodhisattvas; the latter is that of the Buddhas.

Q: By what means can they be attained?

A: The means for gaining the Bodhisattvas' Vehicle are those of the Mahāyāna. Attaining to it and thenceforth remaining so free from discursive thought that even the concept of 'a means' no longer exists for you—such utter tranquillity[31] with nothing to be added to it, nothing to be taken away, is called attainment of the Supreme Vehicle, which is that of the Buddhas!

*   *   *

17. Q: The Mahāparinirvāṇa Sūtra says: 'Excess of dhyāna (ting) over wisdom (hui) provides no way out from primordial ignorance (avidyā), while excess of wisdom over dhyāna leads to piling up false views; but, when dhyāna and wisdom function on the same level, that is what we call deliverance.' What does it all mean?

A: Wisdom means the ability to distinguish every sort of good and evil; dhyāna means that, though making these distinctions, you remain wholly unaffected by love or aversion for them[32]—such is the explanation of dhyāna and wisdom functioning on the same level.

* * *

18. Q: That sūtra also says: 'No words, nothing to say— this is called dhyāna.' But can we also speak of being in dhyāna while we are engaged in talking?

A: My definition of dhyāna just now referred to that perpetual dhyāna which is unaffected by speech or silence. Why? Since the Nature of dhyāna functions even while we are engaged in speaking or in making distinctions, our speech and those distinctions also pertain to dhyāna. Similarly, when we contemplate forms with our minds in a state of voidness, the voidness persists as much during the act of regarding those forms as when we are neither speaking nor engaged in any other kind of discursive activity. The same applies to our seeing, hearing, feeling and consciousness. How so? Because, as our own Nature is void, it remains so in all situations; being void, it is free from attachment, and it is this detachment which makes possible the simultaneous functioning of dhyāna and wisdom on the same level. All Bodhisattvas employ this method of universalizing voidness, which enables them to attain the final Goal. Therefore is it written: 'When dhyāna and wisdom function on the same level, that is what we call deliverance.' Now I shall give you a further example in order to clarify this, so as to awaken your understanding and set your doubts at rest. Take the case of a bright mirror. When it is reflecting something, does its brightness waver? No, it does not. And when it is not reflecting something, does its brightness waver, then? No. But why is this so? It is unwavering whether an object is present or not because it has the property of reflecting without any sensation being experienced. And so? Where no sensation is present there can be neither movement nor absence of movement. Or take the case of the sunlight. Do the sunbeams waver when they shine upon the earth? No! Or do they waver when they do not encounter the earth? No, they do not. Why? Because they are devoid of sensation. That they do not waver whether they encounter something or not is due to their property of shining without experiencing sensation. The quality of being able to reflect (or shine)[33] pertains to wisdom, while that of perfect steadiness pertains to dhyāna. It is the Bodhisattvas' employment of this method of equalizing dhyāna and wisdom which enables them to attain Sambodhi (Supreme Enlightenment). Therefore is it written: 'When dhyāna and wisdom are on the same level, that is what we call deliverance.' However, when I spoke just now of absence of sensation, I meant freedom from ordinary sensations, not from holy sensation.

Q: How do they differ?

A: Ordinary sensations are those involving duality of feeling; holy sensation pertains to realization of the voidness of opposites.

*   *   *

19. Q: The sūtra says: 'The path of words and speech is cut off; the mind's activities cease.' What does this mean?

A: Words and speech are to reveal the Dharma's meaning; but, once that meaning is understood, speech is discarded. Meaning is immaterial; that which is immaterial is Tao (Truth), and Tao is inexpressible. Hence 'the path of words and speech is cut off'. By 'the mind's activities cease' is meant that, upon actual realization of the Dharma's significance, no further contemplation is required. That which lies beyond our contemplation is the Uncreate. Being uncreated, the nature of all appearances is void. Because their nature is (seen to be) void, all their concurrent causes are eradicated, and that eradication involves the cessation of the mind's activities.

*   *   *

20. Q: What is Suchness (Ju-ju, Bhutatathatā)?

A: Suchness signifies immutability. Since mind is immutable (jên-ju, absolute), we term it Suchness. Hence it can be known that all the Buddhas of the past attained Enlightenment by conducting themselves in accord with this immutability. With the Buddhas of the present it is likewise and so will it be with the Buddhas of the future. Since all practice, whether past, present or future, culminates in the same attainment of Enlightenment, it is called the attainment of Suchness. The Vimalakīrti Nirdeśa Sūtra says: 'Thus has it ever been with all the Buddhas; thus will it be with Maitreya[34] and with every other sentient being as well.' Why so? Because the Buddha-Nature is eternally and uninterruptedly self-existent.

*   *   *

21. Q: Does the (teaching concerning the) identity of matter and the immaterial (void), and that of ordinary and holy, pertain to the doctrine of sudden Illumination?

A: Yes.

Q: What do you mean by the identity of matter and void and of ordinary and holy?

A: When mind is stained by attachment, materiality is there; when it is free from stain, immateriality is there. Stained mind is ordinary and unstained mind holy. The Absolute is self-existent, which implies the identity of the immaterial and matter; but, since the latter is not discoverable, it is in fact immaterial. Here, we are using 'immaterial' with reference to the void nature of form, not to mean (the kind of) voidness which would result from form's annihilation.[35] Similarly, we are using 'material' with reference to the nature of the immaterial, which exists of itself, not in the sense that the material can be matter (as ordinarily understood).

*   *   *

22. Q: What are the exhaustibles and the inexhaustibles mentioned in the sūtra?

A: On account of the void nature of all dualities, when seeing and hearing no longer take place, that is exhaustion —meaning the end of passions (āsravaksaya). Inexhaustible connotes the uncreated substance complete with marvellous functions as numerous as the sands of the Ganges. These functions respond to all the needs (of sentient beings) without occasioning the smallest diminution of substance. Such, then, are the exhaustibles and inexhaustibles mentioned in the sūtras.[36]

Q: Are the exhaustibles and inexhaustibles really identical or are they different things?

A: In substance they are one, but they are spoken of separately.

Q: Yet, if they are one in substance, why should they be spoken of separately?

A: 'One' denotes the substance of speech, and speech

is a function of that substance; it is employed as circumstances require. That is why they are said to be of the same substance but spoken of separately. We may liken this to the fact that, although only the one sun appears in the sky above, its reflections are caught by water held by many different receptacles, so that each of those receptacles 'contains a sun' and every 'sun' is both complete in itself and yet identical with the sun in the sky. Therefore, although the suns are of the same substance, they are spoken of separately with reference to the various receptacles. Hence (things of) the same substance are spoken of differently. Moreover, although every one of the suns manifested below is perfect and entire, the sun in the sky is not in the least diminished by them—hence the term inexhaustible.

Q: A sūtra speaks of 'no coming into existence and no ceasing to exist'. To what sort of dharmas (phenomena) do these words apply?

A: They mean the not coming into existence of unwholesome phenomena and the never ceasing to exist of wholesome phenomena.[37]

Q: What are wholesome and unwholesome phenomena?

A: A mind stained by attachments and leaking[38] is unwholesome; a mind freed from these characteristics is wholesome. It is only when no stains or leaking occur that unwholesomeness does not arise; and, when freedom from stains and leaking is attained, there is purity, perfection and brilliance—a deep, everlasting and unwavering stillness. This is what is meant by wholesome phenomena not ceasing to be; it explains the term 'no coming into existence or ceasing to exist'.

*   *   *

E

23. Q: The Precepts of the Bodhisattvas says: 'When sentient beings observe the Buddha Precept, they enter upon the status of Buddhahood—a status identical with Full Enlightenment—and thereby they become true sons of the Buddhas.' What does this mean?

A: The Buddha Precept denotes perfect purity[39] of mind. If someone undertakes the practice of purity, and thereby attains a mind unmoved by sensory perceptions, we speak of him as one who observes the Buddha Precept. All the Buddhas up to this day have practised purity unmoved by sensory perceptions and it was by means of this that they attained Buddhahood. In these days, if someone undertakes its practice, his merit is equal to and does not differ from that of the Buddhas; hence he is said to have entered upon the status of Buddhahood. Illumination thus obtained is precisely the Illumination of a Buddha, so such a man's status is said to be identical with Full Enlightenment. He really is a son of the Buddhas and his pure mind begets wisdom. He whose wisdom is pure is called a son of the Buddhas or 'this Buddha son'.

*   *   *

24. Q: As to the Buddhas[40] and the Dharma, which of them anteceded the other? If the Dharma came first, how can there have been a Buddha to preach it; but, if a Buddha came first, then what doctrine led to his attainment?

A: The Buddhas anteceded the Dharma in one sense, but came after it in another.

Q: How is that possible?

A: If you mean the Quiescent Dharma, then the Dharma anteceded the Buddhas; but, if you mean the written or spoken Dharma, then it was the Buddhas who came first and the Dharma which followed them. How so? Because every one of the Buddhas attained Buddhahood by means of the Quiescent Dharma—in that sense, the Dharma anteceded them. The 'Teacher of all the Buddhas' mentioned in the sūtra is the Dharma; it was not until they had attained Buddhahood that they first embarked upon their detailed exposition of the Twelve Divisions of the Sūtras for the purpose of converting sentient beings. When these sentient beings follow and practise the Dharma preached by previous Buddhas, thereby attaining Buddhahood, that is also a case of the Dharma anteceding the Buddha.

*　　　*　　　*

25. Q: What is meant by 'proficiency in Teaching but not in Transmission'?[41]

A: It refers to those whose words are at variance with their deeds.

Q: And what is meant by 'proficiency in Transmission and also in Teaching'?

A: It refers to people whose words are confirmed by their deeds.

*　　　*　　　*

26. Q: What is meant by 'the reachable not reached' and by 'the unreachable reached'?

A: By 'the reachable not reached' is meant speech not supported by deeds; by 'the unreachable reached' is meant deeds performing what speech fails to reach; and, when both speech and deeds attain the Goal, this is 'complete reaching' or 'double reaching'.

*　　　*　　　*

27. Q: Please explain the two statements: 'The Buddha-Dharma neither annihilates the worldly (yu wei) nor gets bogged down in the transcendental (wu wei).'[42]

A: The first means that the Buddha never rejected any thing phenomenal from the moment when he first determined upon his quest up to the time when he achieved Enlightenment beneath the Bodhi Tree and from then up to his entrance into Parinirvāṇa beneath the twin sāla trees.[43] This is 'non-annihilation of the worldly'. The other statement means that, although he achieved absence of thought, he never looked upon this as an attainment; that, although he reached immaterial and non-active Bodhi and Nirvāṇa, he never held that these states marked an attainment. This is what is meant by 'not getting bogged down in the transcendental'.

*   *   *

28. Q: Is there really a hell?[44]

A: There is and there is not.

Q: How so?

A: In that our minds have constructed many sorts of evil karma, there is hell; but, since everyone's self-nature is void, for those whose minds have been freed of attachment's stains there can be no hell.

Q: Do evil-doers possess the Buddha-Nature?

A: Yes, they have it too.

Q: Then, if they too have this Nature, does it enter hell with them or not?

A: It does not enter with them.

Q: But, when they enter hell, where is their Buddha-Nature?

A: It also enters hell.[45]

Q: That being so, while they are undergoing punishment there, does their Buddha-Nature share the punishment?

A: No. Although the Buddha-Nature remains with these people while they are in hell, it is the individuals themselves who suffer; the Buddha-Nature is fundamentally beyond punishment.

Q: Yet, if they enter together, how can the Buddha-Nature not suffer?

A: Sentient beings possess forms and whatsoever has form is subject to formation and destruction;[46] whereas the Buddha-Nature is formless, and, being formless, is immaterial, for which reason it is the very nature of the void itself and cannot be destroyed. Were someone to make a pile of faggots in a vacuum, the faggots could come to harm but not the vacuum. In this analogy, the vacuum symbolizes the Buddha-Nature and the faggots represent sentient beings. Therefore it is written: 'They enter together but do not suffer together.'

*   *   *

29. Q: Regarding the quotation 'Transform the eight states of consciousness (parijñāna)[47] into the four Buddha-Wisdoms[48] and bind the four Buddha-Wisdoms to form the Trikāya',[49] which of the eight states of consciousness must be combined to form one Buddha-Wisdom and which of them will each become a Buddha-Wisdom in itself?

A: Sight, hearing, smell, taste and touch are the five states of consciousness which together form the Perfecting Wisdom. The intellect or sixth state of consciousness alone becomes the Profound Observing Wisdom. Discriminative awareness or the seventh state of consciousness alone becomes the Universal Wisdom. The storehouse of consciousness or eighth state alone becomes the Great Mirror Wisdom.

Q: Do these four Wisdoms really differ?

A: In substance they are the same, but they are differently named.

Q: Yet, if they are one in substance, why do their names differ? Or, allowing that their names are given according to circumstances, what it is that, being of one substance (with the rest), is (nevertheless called) the Great Mirror Wisdom?

A: That which is clearly void and still, bright and imperturbable, is the Great Mirror Wisdom. That which can face defilements without love or aversion arising and which thereby exhibits the non-existent nature of all such dualities is the Universal Wisdom. That which can range the fields of the senses with unexcelled ability to discern things, yet without giving rise to tumultuous thoughts, so that it is fully independent and at ease, is the Profound Observing Wisdom. That which can convert all the senses with their functions of responding to circumstances into correct sensation[50] free from duality is the Perfecting Wisdom.

Q: As to 'Binding the four Buddha-Wisdoms to form the Trikāya', which of them combine to form one Body and which of them each becomes a Body in itself?

A: The Great Mirror Wisdom singly forms the Dharmakāya. The Universal Wisdom singly forms the Sambhogakāya. The Profound Observing Wisdom and the Perfecting Wisdom jointly form the Nirmāṇakāya. These Three Bodies are only named differently to enable unenlightened people to see more clearly. Once the principle is understood, there will be no more Three Bodies with functions responding to various needs. Why? Formless in substance and by nature, they are established in the basically impermanent,[51] which is not their own (true basis) at all.

*   *   *

30. Q: What is meant by perceiving the real Buddhakāya?[52]

A: It means no longer perceiving anything as existing or not existing.

Q: But what is the actual meaning of that definition?

A: Existence is a term used in contradistinction to non-existence, while the latter is used in opposition to the former. Unless you begin by accepting the first concept as valid, the other cannot stand. Similarly, without the concept of non-existence, how can that of existence have meaning? These two owe their being to mutual dependence and pertain to the realm of birth and death. It is just by avoiding such dual perception that we may come to behold the real Buddhakāya.[53]

Q: If even the concepts of existence and non-existence are invalid, how can that of a real Buddhakāya have validity?

A: Only because you are asking about it! When such questions are not asked, the concept of a Buddhakāya is not valid. Why? Take the case of a mirror; confronted by objects, it reflects them; unconfronted, it reflects nothing.

*   *   *

31. Q: What is meant by 'being never apart from the Buddha'?[54]

A: Having a mind freed from the going and coming of concepts, its stillness unaffected by environmental forms so that it remains eternally void and motionless—this is being never apart from the Buddha.

*　　　　*　　　　*

32. Q: What is the meaning of the transcendental (wu wei, unconditioned, asaṁskṛta)?

A: It is worldly (yu wei, conditioned, saṁskṛta).[55]

Q: I enquired about the transcendental. Why do you say it is worldly?

A: Worldly is a term valid only in contradistinction to transcendental. The latter derives its meaning from the former. If you do not accept the one as a valid concept, the other cannot be retained. But if you are speaking of the REAL Transcendental, that pertains neither to the worldly nor to the transcendental. Yes, the Real Transcendental is like that! Why? The Diamond Sūtra says: 'If their minds grasp the Dharma, they will still cling to the notion of an ego (a being and a life); if their minds grasp the Non-Dharma, they will still cling to the notion of an ego (a being and a life). Therefore, we should not grasp at and hold on to the notions either of Dharma or of Not-Dharma.' This is holding to the true Dharma. If you understand this doctrine, that is true deliverance—that, indeed, is reaching the gate of non-duality.

*　　　　*　　　　*

33. Q: What is the significance of the term 'middle way'?

A: It signifies the extremes.

Q: I enquired about the middle way; why do you say it signifies the extremes?

A: Extremes are only valid in contradistinction to the

middle way. If at first you do not postulate extremes, from what can you derive the concept of a middle way? This middle you are talking about was first used in relation to extremes. Hence we should realize that middle and extremes owe their existence to their mutual dependence and that all of them are transient. The same rule applies equally to the skandhas—form, sensation, perceptions, impulses (or volitions) and consciousness.[56]

*   *   *

34. Q: What are these things which we call the five skandhas?

A: The propensity to allow the forms we encounter to set their stain upon us, thereby arousing forms in our minds, is called the skandha of form. As this leads to the reception of the eight winds[57] which encourage the piling up of wrong notions, sensations are aroused,[58] and this is called the skandha of sensation. Thereupon, the deluded mind takes to perceiving (individual sensations) and perception is aroused, and this is called the skandha of perception. This leads to the piling up of impulses (based on likes and dislikes) and this is called the skandha of impulse (or volition). Accordingly, within the undifferentiated substance, error gives rise to the notion of plurality and countless attachments are formed, whereat false consciousness (or wrong understanding) arises, and this is called the skandha of consciousness. It is thus that we define the five skandhas.

*   *   *

35. Q: A sūtra says that there are twenty-five factors of existence. What are they?

A: This term refers to our having to undergo future in-
carnations—or rebirths taking place within the six realms.[59]
Owing to the delusions filling our minds during the present
life, we sentient beings have become closely bound by all
sorts of karma and will receive rebirth in exact accordance
with our karmic state. Hence the term reincarnation. However, if during a given existence there are people determined upon doing their utmost to gain deliverance, and
who thereby attain to the state of no rebirth, they will leave
the three worlds for ever and never more have to be reborn. This implies attainment of the Dharmakāya in the
absolute sense of Buddhakāya.

Q: How do these twenty-five factors of existence differ
from one another?

A: Their basic substance is one. However, when we name
them in accordance with their various functions, there
appear to be twenty-five of them. This figure really connotes the ten evils, the ten virtues and the five skandhas.

Q: What are the ten evils and the ten virtues?

A: The ten evils are killing, stealing, licentiousness,
lying, voluptuous speech, slander, coarse language, covet-
ousness, anger and false views.[60] The ten virtues may be
simply defined as absence of the ten evils.[61]

*   *   *

36. Q: A little while ago you spoke of refraining from
thinking (nien), but you did not finish your explanation.[62]

A: It means not fixing your mind upon anything anywhere, but totally withdrawing it from the phenomena
surrounding you, so that even the thought (szŭ) of seeking
for something does not remain; it means that your mind,

confronted by all the forms composing your environment, remains placid and motionless. This abstaining from all thought whatever is called REAL thought; but to keep on thinking is deluded thinking and certainly not the right way to think. Why is that? A sūtra says: 'If you teach people to entertain the six meritorious thoughts,[63] that is called teaching them to think in the wrong way.' So, even entertaining those six thoughts is termed deluded thinking, while abstaining from them is known as real thought. A sūtra says: 'O virtuous one, it is through abiding in the Dharma of No Thought that we obtain this golden colour and these thirty-two bodily marks of Buddhahood which emit an effulgent radiance that penetrates the entire universe.' Such inconceivable merits even the Buddhas cannot describe in full; how much the less can the devotees of other Vehicles know about them! Those who achieve abstention from thought[64] are naturally able to enter upon the Buddha-Perception, for their six senses can no longer stain their minds. Such an attainment is called entering the Treasury of the Buddhas, also known as the Treasury of the Dharma, which enables you to perform the Dharmas of all Buddhas. How can that be so? Because of abstention from thought. The same sūtra says: 'All Buddhas are produced by this sūtra.'

Q: If we esteem absence of thought, how can the notion of 'entering upon Buddha-Perception' have any validity?

A: Its validity stems from absence of thought. How so? A sūtra says: 'All things take their stand upon the basis of non-abiding.' It also says: 'Take the case of a bright mirror; though it contains no forms, it can manifest a myriad forms.' Why is this? It is because of its brightness (stainless clarity) that it is able to reflect them. You disciples, if your minds are stainless, will thereby be freed from entertaining erroneous thoughts; the stirring of your minds by the notion of self and others will vanish; there will be nothing but purity (stainlessness) on account of which you will become capable of unlimited perception. Sudden Illumination means deliverance WHILE STILL IN THIS LIFE. How shall I make you understand that? You may be compared to lion-cubs, which are genuine lions from the time of their birth;[65] for, with those who undertake to become suddenly Illumined, it is just like that. The moment they practise it, they enter the Buddha-Stage, just as the shoots put forth by bamboos in spring will have grown to resemble the parent plants without the least difference remaining even before spring has departed. Why so? Because the minds of these people are void. Likewise, they who undertake sudden Illumination cut off erroneous thoughts at a stroke, thereby eliminating the duality of selfness and otherness, so that perfect voidness and stillness supervene—thereby parity with the Buddhas is achieved without one jot of difference remaining. Therefore it is written that the most ordinary beings are profoundly holy.[66] Those who undertake sudden Illumination transcend the three realms of existence within this very life! As a sūtra says: 'Transcend the world from its very midst; enter Nirvāṇa ere ridding yourselves of Saṃsāra's moil.'[67] If you do not employ this method of sudden Illumination, you will be like a jackal following and imitating a lion but unable to become a lion[68] even after hundreds and thousands of aeons.

Q: Is the nature of the Absolute (Chên-ju) a true void, or not really void? To describe it as not void is to imply that it has form; yet to speak of it as void implies extinction (mere nothingness) and what would then be left for sentient beings to rely on in their practice for attaining deliverance?

A: The nature of the Absolute is void and yet not void. How so? The marvellous 'substance' of the Absolute, having neither form nor shape, is therefore undiscoverable; hence it is void. Nevertheless, that immaterial, formless 'substance' contains functions as numerous as the sands of the Ganges, functions which respond unfailingly to circumstances, so it is also described as not void.[69] A sūtra says: 'Understand the one point and a thousand others will accordingly grow clear; misunderstand that one and ten thousand delusions will encompass you. He who holds to that one has no more problems to solve.' This is the great marvellous awakening to the Way (Truth). As one of the sūtras says: 'The myriad forms dense and close bear the imprint of a single Dharma.' How then can so many sorts of views arise from the One Dharma? All these karmic forces are rooted in activity. If, instead of pacifying our minds, we rely on Scriptures to achieve Enlightenment, we are undertaking the impossible. Ourselves deceived, deceiving others, our mutual downfall is assured. Strive on! Strive on! Explore this teaching most thoroughly! Just let things happen without making any response and keep your minds from dwelling on anything whatsoever; for he who can do this thereby enters Nirvāṇa. Attained, then, is the condition of no rebirth, otherwise called the gate of non-duality, the end of strife, the samādhi of universality.[70] Why so? Because it is ultimate purity. As it is free from the duality of selfness and otherness, it no longer gives rise to love and hatred. When all relativities are seen as non-existent, naught remains to be perceived.[71] Thus is the undiscoverable Bhūtatathatā revealed. This treatise of mine is not for the sceptic, but for those sharing the same view and following the same line of conduct. You ought first to discover whether a man is sincere in his faith and qualified to practise it without backsliding before you expound it to him so that he can be awakened to its meaning. I have written this treatise for the sake of those having a karmic affinity with it. I seek neither fame nor wealth. I desire only to emulate the Buddhas who preached their thousands of sūtras and countless śāstras just for the sake of sentient beings lost in delusion. Since their mental activities vary, appropriate teachings are given to suit individual cases of perverse views; hence the great variety of doctrines. You should know that setting forth the principle of deliverance in its entirety amounts only to this—WHEN THINGS HAPPEN, MAKE NO RESPONSE: KEEP YOUR MINDS FROM DWELLING ON ANYTHING WHATSOEVER: KEEP THEM FOR EVER STILL AS THE VOID AND UTTERLY PURE (WITHOUT STAIN): AND THEREBY SPONTANEOUSLY ATTAIN DELIVERANCE. Oh do not seek for empty fame, mouthing forth talk of the Absolute with minds like those of apes! When talk contradicts actions, that is known as self-deception; it will lead to your falling headlong into evil states of rebirth. Seek not fame and happiness in this lifetime at the cost of unenlightenment and suffering for long aeons to come. Strive on! Strive on! Sentient beings must save themselves; the Buddhas cannot do it for them. If they could, since there have already been Buddhas as numerous as grains of dust,[72] every single being must by now have been saved; then how is it that you and I are still being tossed upon the waves of life and death instead of having become Buddhas? Do please realize that sentient beings have to save themselves and that the Buddhas cannot do it for them. Strive on! Strive on! Do it for yourselves. Place no reliance upon the powers of other Buddhas.[73] As the sūtra says: 'Those who seek the Dharma do not find it merely by clinging to the Buddhas.'

*   *   *

37. Q: In the coming generation, there will be many followers of mixed beliefs; how are we to live side by side with them?

A: Share the light with them, but do not share their karmas. Although you may be staying with them, your minds will not dwell in the same place as theirs. There is a sūtra which says: 'Though it follows the current of circumstances, its nature is unchanging.' As to those other students of the Way, you are all studying the Way for the sake of that great cause—liberation; so, while never despising those who have not studied the Dharma, you should respect those who are studying it as you would respect the Buddha. Do not vaunt your own virtues nor envy the ability of others. Examine your own actions; do not hold up the faults of others. Thus nowhere will you encounter obstruction and you will naturally enjoy happiness. I will summarize all this in the form of a gāthā:

> Forbearance is the best of ways;
> But first dismiss both 'self' and 'other'.
> When things occur, make no response—
> And thus achieve true Bodhikāya.[74]

The Diamond Sūtra says: 'If a Bodhisattva is thoroughly versed in the doctrine of the unreality of the ego and of all dharmas (things), the Tathāgata will call him a true Bodhisattva.' It is also said that 'he who does not accept anything has nothing to reject; he is free of Saṁsāra for ever. He whose mind dwells on nothing whatsoever is called a son of the Buddha.' The Mahāparinirvāṇa Sūtra says: 'When the Tathāgata attained Nirvāṇa, he freed himself from Saṁsāra for ever.' Here are some more gāthās:

So wholly good my present state of mind
That men's revilement cannot stir my ire.
No word shall pass my lips of 'right' and 'wrong'—
Nirvāṇa and Saṁsāra form one Way—
For I have learnt to reach that mind of mine
Which basically transcends both right and wrong.
Erroneous, discriminating thoughts
Reveal the worldling who has still to learn.
I urge the errant folk of Kaliyug[75]
To rid their minds of every useless straw.

How vast indeed my present state of mind—
My wordless unconcern ensures its calm.
At ease and free, my liberation won,
I roam at will without impediment.
In wordless silence all my days are passed,
My every thought fixed on the Noumenal.
In gazing on the Way, I am at ease
And unaffected by Saṁsāra's round.

So marvellous my present state of mind,
I need intrude no longer on the world,
Where splendour is illusion and a cheat;
The simplest clothes and coarsest food suffice.
On meeting worldly men, I scarcely speak,
And so they say that I am dull of wit.
Without, I have what seems a dullard's stare;
Within, my crystal clarity of mind
Soundlessly tallies with Rāhul's hidden way[76]
Which worldly folk like you have yet to learn.

For fear that you may still be unable to understand the real principle of deliverance, I shall demonstrate it to you once more.

*   *   *

38. Q: The Vimalakīrti Nirdeśa Sūtra says: 'Whosoever desires to reach the Pure Land must first purify his mind.' What is the meaning of this purifying of the mind?

A: It means purifying it to the point of ultimate purity.

Q: But what does that mean?

A: It is a state beyond purity and impurity.

Q: Please explain it further.

A: Purity pertains to a mind which dwells upon nothing whatsoever. To attain to this without so much as a thought of purity arising is called absence of purity; and to achieve that without giving it a thought is to be free from absence of purity also.

*   *   *

39. Q: For followers of the Way, what constitutes realization of the Goal?

A: Realization must be ultimate realization.

Q: And what is that?

A: Ultimate realization means being free from both realization and absence of realization.[77]

Q: What does that mean?

A: Realization means remaining unstained by sights, sounds and other sense-perceptions from without, and inwardly possessing minds in which no erroneous thinking takes place. To achieve this without giving it a thought is called absence of realization; and to achieve the latter without giving that a thought either is called freedom from absence of realization.

*   *   *

40. Q: What is meant by 'a mind delivered'?

A: Having a mind free from the concepts of delivered and undelivered is called real deliverance. This is what the

F

Diamond Sūtra means by the words: 'Even the Dharma must be cast aside, how much more so the not-Dharma!' Here, Dharma implies existence and not-Dharma implies non-existence—disengagement from both of which results in true deliverance.

*　　　*　　　*

41. Q: What is realization of Truth (Tao)?

A: It means ultimate realization.

Q: What is that?

A: Ultimate realization is beyond realization and non-realization.

Q: And what is ultimate voidness?

A: Ultimate voidness is beyond voidness and non-voidness.[78]

Q: And what is the fixed Bhūtatathatā (Absolute)?

A: The Bhūtatathatā's fixity is neither fixed nor unfixed. The Diamond Sūtra says: 'There is no FIXED Dharma called Anuttara-Samyak-Saṁbodhi (Supreme Enlightenment) and there is no fixed Dharma which the Tathāgata can expound.' This is what another sūtra means by: 'When meditating on the void, perception of the void should not be taken as realization.' This means abstention from the thought of voidness. Similarly, although we practise fixing the mind, we do not regard (success in this practice) as realization, because we entertain no thought of fixity. Likewise, although we attain purity, we do not regard it as realization, because we entertain no thought of purity. Even when we attain to fixed concentration, to purity and to the state of letting the mind dwell upon nothing whatsoever, if we permit any thought of our having made progress to enter our minds, that thought will be an erroneous thought and we shall be caught in a net—that cannot be called deliverance! Moreover, if after attaining to all this we experience a lively awareness of being at ease and independent (of all conditioning factors and so on), we must not take this for realization or suppose that deliverance can be won by thinking in this way. As the sūtra says: 'Allowing the concept of progress to enter our minds is not progress but error; whereas, if we keep our minds free from error, progress is unlimited.'

*   *   *

42. Q: What is the middle way?

A: It is without middle or extremes.

Q: What are the two extremes?

A. They are that-mindedness (pi hsin) and this-mindedness (tzŭ hsin).

Q: What do those terms mean?

A: Being ensnared from without by forms and sounds is that-mindedness; allowing erroneous thoughts to arise within is this-mindedness. Being unstained from without by forms is called freedom from that-mindedness; permitting no erroneous thoughts to arise within is called freedom from this-mindedness. Such is the meaning of 'no extremes'. And, if your minds are without extremes, how can there be a middle? Reaching this state is called the 'middle way' or the true Way of the Tathāgatas by which completely awakened men reach deliverance. A sūtra says: 'The void is without middle or extremes; with the Buddhakāya it is also thus.' The voidness of all forms implies mind dwelling upon nothing whatsoever; and the latter implies the void nature of all forms—these are two ways of saying the same thing. This is the doctrine of the unreality of form, also called the doctrine of the non-existence of form. If you people reject 'mind dwelling upon nothing whatsoever', then Bodhi (Enlightenment), still and passionless Nirvāṇa and perception of your real nature through dhyāna-samādhi will all be closed to you. It is just by not allowing your minds to dwell upon anything whatsoever that you will perceive your own nature, whenever you practise attainment of Bodhi, deliverance, Nirvāṇa, dhyāna-samādhi or the six pāramitās. Why so? The Diamond Sūtra says: 'Realizing that there is not the smallest thing to be attained is called Anuttara-Samyak-Saṁbodhi (Supreme Enlightenment).'

*   *   *

43. Q: If we have performed all (good) deeds successfully, shall we receive a prediction of our future Buddhahood?[79]

A: No.

Q: If we have gained ultimate achievement by refraining from the practice of any dharma (method) whatsoever, shall we receive that prediction?

A: No.

Q: In that case, by what dharma is that prediction to be obtained?

A: It is obtainable when you cease (clinging to) deeds and to no deeds. Why so? The Vimalakīrti Nirdeśa Sūtra says: 'The nature and the phenomenal expression of all deeds are both impermanent.' According to the Mahā-parinirvāṇa Sūtra: 'The Buddha said to Kāśyapa: "There is no such thing as permanence of the totality of phenomenal activity." ' You must just avoid letting your minds dwell upon anything whatsoever, which implies (being un-concerned about) either deeds or no deeds—that is what we call receiving a prediction of Buddhahood. What I mean by not letting the mind dwell upon anything whatsoever is keeping your minds free from hatred and love. This means that you must be able to see attractive things without love for them arising in your minds, which is termed having minds free from love; and also that you must be able to see repulsive things without hatred for them arising in your minds, which is termed having minds free from hatred. When these two are absent, the mind is unstained and the nature of forms is seen as void. Perception of the voidness of their nature leads to the cutting off of con- current causes and thus to spontaneous deliverance. You must examine this thoroughly. If the meaning is not brilliantly clear to you, hasten to ask your questions. Do not allow the hours to pass in vain. If you people put your trust in this teaching and act accordingly, without being delivered, I shall gladly take your places in hell for the whole of my existence. If I have deceived you, may I be reborn in a place where lions, tigers and wolves will devour my flesh! But, if you do not put your faith in this teaching, and do not practise it diligently, that will be because you do not understand it. Once you have lost a human body, you will not obtain another for millions of aeons. Strive on! Strive on! It is absolutely vital that you come to understand.

THE TSUNG CHING RECORD
OF THE ZEN MASTER HUI HAI
ALSO KNOWN AS THE GREAT PEARL

*A collection of dialogues recorded by the Monk Tsung Ching of
Hua Yen Monastery in the city of Yü*

(Throughout Part Two 'M' stands for 'The Master' while
'Q' and 'A' stand for the questions and answers of others.)

1. When the Master first arrived in Kiangsi to pay his
respects to Ma Tsu, the latter enquired: 'From where have
you come?'

'From the Great Cloud Monastery at Yüeh Chou,'
answered the Master.

Q: 'What do you hope to gain by coming here?'

M: 'I have come seeking the Buddha-Dharma.'

To this Ma Tsu replied: 'Instead of looking to the
treasure house which is your very own, you have left home
and gone wandering far away. What for? I have absolutely
nothing here at all.[80] What is this Buddha-Dharma that
you seek?'

Whereat the Master prostrated himself and enquired:
'Please tell me to what you alluded when you spoke of a
treasure house of my very own.'

A: 'That which asked the question is your treasure
house. It contains absolutely everything you need and lacks

nothing at all. It is there for you to use freely, so why this vain search for something outside yourself?'

No sooner were these words spoken than the Master received a great Illumination and recognized his own mind! Beside himself with joy, he hastened to show his gratitude by prostrating himself again.

The Master spent the next six years in attendance upon Ma Tsu; but, as his first Teacher—the one responsible for his admission to the monastic order—was growing old, he had to return to Yüeh Chou to look after him. There he lived a retired life, concealing his abilities and outwardly appearing somewhat mad. It was at this time that he composed his śāstra—*A Treatise Setting Forth the Essential Gateway to Truth by Means of Instantaneous Awakening*. Later this book was stolen by Hsüan Yen, a disciple of his brother-in-the-Dharma, who brought it from the Yangtse region and showed it to Ma Tsu. Ma Tsu, after reading it carefully, declared to his disciples:

'In Yüeh Chou there is now a great pearl; its lustre penetrates everywhere freely and without obstruction.'

Now it happened that the assembly included a monk who knew that the Master had, in lay-life, been surnamed Chu (a word identical in sound with the word for pearl). In great excitement he hastened to communicate this information to some other monks, who went in a group to Yüeh Chou to call on the Master and follow him. Thenceforward the Master was called the Great Pearl.

(Note inserted in the Chinese text: The Master Hui Hai, Ocean of Wisdom, was a native of Chien Chou.[81] He was received into the Order by the Venerable Tao Chih in the Great Cloud Monastery at Yüeh Chou.)

*   *   *

2. Once the Master began his daily address to his disciples by saying: 'I am no Ch'an adept; indeed, I have not a single thing to offer anyone, so I must not keep you standing here longer. Go and take a rest.'[82]

In those days the number of people who came to study under him was gradually increasing. As day follows night, they came and pressed him for instruction; he was compelled to answer their questions as soon as asked, thus revealing his unimpeded powers of dialectic. Endless discussions took place with questions and answers following one upon another.

Once a group of Dharma Masters (learned preachers) sought an interview and said: 'We have some questions to ask. Are you prepared to answer them, Master?'

M: 'Yes. The moon is reflected in that deep pond; catch it if you like.'[83]

Q: 'What is the Buddha really like?'

M: 'If that which is facing the limpid pond[84] is not the Buddha, what is it?'

The monks were puzzled by this reply; after a long pause, they enquired again: 'Master, what dharma (doctrine) do you expound in order to liberate others?'

M: 'This poor monk[85] has no dharma by which to liberate others.'

'All Ch'an Masters are of the same stuff!' they exclaimed, whereat the Master asked them:

'What dharmas do you Virtuous Ones expound for liberating others?'

A: 'Oh, we expound the Diamond Sūtra.'

M: 'How many times have you expounded it?'

A: 'More than twenty times.'

M: 'By whom was it spoken?'

To this the monks answered indignantly: 'Master, you

must be joking! Of course you know that it was spoken by the Buddha.'

M: 'Well, that sūtra states: "If someone says the Tathāgata expounds the Dharma, he thereby slanders the Buddha![86] Such a man will never understand what I mean." Now, if you say that it was not expounded by the Buddha, you will thereby belittle that sūtra. Will you Virtuous Ones please let me see what you have to say to that?'

As they made no reply, the Master paused awhile before asking his next question, which was: 'The Diamond Sūtra says: "He who seeks me through outward appearance, or seeks me in sound, treads the heterodox path and cannot perceive the Tathāgata." Tell me, Virtuous Ones, who or what is the Tathāgata?'[87]

A: 'Sir, at this point I find myself utterly deluded.'

M: 'Having never been Illumined, how can you say that you are now deluded?'

So then the monk (who had spoken) asked: 'Will the Venerable Ch'an Master expound the Dharma to us?'

M: 'Though you have expounded the Diamond Sūtra over twenty times, you still do not know the Tathāgata!'

These words caused the monks to prostrate themselves again and to beg the Master to explain further, so he said: 'The Diamond Sūtra states: "The Tathāgata is the Suchness of all dharmas (phenomena)." How can you have forgotten that?'

A: 'Yes, yes—the Suchness of all dharmas.'

M: 'Virtuous Ones, "yes" is also incorrect.'

A: 'On that point the Scripture is very clear. How can ve be wrong?'

M: 'Then, Virtuous Ones, are you that Suchness (too)?'

A: 'Yes, we are.'

M: 'And are plants and rocks the Suchness?'

A: 'They are.'

M: 'Then is the Suchness of you Virtuous Ones the same as the Suchness of plants and rocks?'

A: 'There is no difference.'

M: 'Then how do you Virtuous Ones differ from plants and rocks?'[88]

This silenced the monks for some time, until at last one of them exclaimed with a sigh: 'It is hard to keep our end up in discussions with a man so very much our superior.'

After a considerable pause, they enquired: 'How can Mahāparinirvāṇa be attained?'

M: 'By avoiding all saṁsāric deeds—those which keep you in the round of birth and death.'

Q: 'What deeds are they?'

M: 'Well, seeking Nirvāṇa is a saṁsāric deed. Casting off impurity and clinging to purity is another. Harbouring attainments and proofs of attainment is another, and so is failure to discard rules and precepts.'

Q: 'Please tell us how to achieve deliverance.'

M: 'Never having been bound, you have no need to seek deliverance. Straightforward functioning and straightforward conduct cannot be surpassed.'

'Ah,' exclaimed the monks, 'people like this Venerable Ch'an Master are indeed rare!' Then they bowed their thanks and left.

*   *   *

3. Once a man who practised Ch'an asked the Master: 'It is said that Mind is identical with the Buddha, but which of these is REALLY the Buddha?'

M: 'What do you suppose is NOT the Buddha. Point it out to me!'

As there was no answer, the Master added: 'If you comprehend (the mind), the Buddha is omnipresent to you; but, if you do not awaken to it, you will remain astray and distant from him for ever.'[89]

*   *   *

4. A Master of the Vinaya Sect named Fa Ming once remarked: 'You Ch'an Masters do a lot of tumbling about in the emptiness of the void.'

M: 'On the contrary, Venerable Sir, it is you who tumble a lot in the emptiness of the void.'

'How can that be?' exclaimed Fa Ming in astonishment.

M: 'The Scriptures are just words—mere ink and paper —and everything of that sort is just an empty device. All those words and phrases are based on something people once heard—they are naught but emptiness. You, Venerable Sir, cling to the mere letter of the doctrine, so of course you tumble about in the void.'

Q: 'And do you Ch'an Masters not tumble in the void?'

M: 'We do not.'

Q: 'How not?'

A: 'All those writings are the products of wisdom; and, where wisdom's mighty function operates, how can there be tumbling about in the void?'

'Ah,' replied Fa Ming. 'From this we know that he for whom there is a single dharma (doctrine) of which he has not grasped the meaning cannot be called a Hsi-Ta (Siddham).'

'Venerable Sir!' exclaimed our Master. 'You not only tumble about in the void; you even misuse Buddhist terminology!'

'What term have I misused?' cried Fa Ming, flushing angrily.

M: 'Why, Venerable Sir, you are even unable to distinguish between a Chinese word and an Indian word, so how can you manage to preach?'

Q: 'Will the Venerable Ch'an Master point out my mistake?'

M: 'Surely you must know that Hsi-Ta (Siddham) is a name for the Sanskrit alphabet?'

Though the Vinaya Master then realized his mistake, he was still blazing with anger.[90]

Fa Ming enquired again: 'The Sūtras, Vinaya and Śāstras[91] are all the teaching of the Buddha. If we read them, recite them, have faith in what they teach, and act accordingly, how can we fail to come face to face with our real nature?'

M: 'All this is like a dog chasing after a lump of flesh or a lion devouring a man. The Sūtras, Vinaya and the Śāstras disclose the function of self-nature—reading and reciting them are mere phenomena arising from that nature.'

Q: 'Had Amitābha Buddha parents and a surname?'[92]

M: 'Yes. Amitābha Buddha was surnamed Kauśika. His father's name was Candra-Uttara and his mother was called Surpassing Beauty.'

Q: 'From which Scripture does this information come?'

M: 'From the *Collection of Dhāraṇī.*'

At this Fa Ming bowed his thanks and departed with expressions of admiration.

*　　　*　　　*

5. A certain Tripiṭaka Master once enquired: 'Do changes occur within the Absolute (Bhūtatathatā?)'

M: 'Yes, they do.'

'Venerable Master,' he replied, 'you are wrong.' Whereat the Master asked him a question as follows:

'Does the Tripiṭaka Master possess the Bhūtatathatā?'

A: 'Yes.'

M: 'Well, if you hold that it undergoes no changes, you must be a very ignorant sort of monk. Surely you must have heard that a learned man can transform the three poisons into the three cumulative precepts;[93] he can transmute the six sense-perceptions into the six divine perceptions; he can transform defilements (kleśa) into Bodhi and primordial ignorance into highest Wisdom (Mahāprajñā). So, if you suppose the Absolute incapable of change, then you—a Master of the Tripiṭaka—are really a follower of the heterodox sect which holds that things happen spontaneously (i.e. not as a result of the law of causality).'

A: 'If you put it that way, then the Absolute does undergo changes.'

M: 'Yet your holding that the Absolute does undergo changes is equally heretical.'

A: 'Venerable Master, first you said that the Absolute does undergo changes and now you say that it does not. What, then, is exactly the right answer?'

M: 'Someone who has clearly perceived his own nature, which may be likened to a Maṇi-pearl reflecting all appearances, will be right if he says that the Absolute does undergo changes and equally right in saying that it does not. On the other hand, anyone who has not seen his own nature will, upon hearing of the changing Absolute, cling to the concept of mutability; or, upon hearing that the Absolute is unchanging, he will grasp at the concept of immutability.'

'Ah, so it is true,' exclaimed the Tripiṭaka Master,

'that the Southern Ch'an Sect really is too deep to fathom!'[94]

* * *

6. Once a Taoist, happening to pass by, asked: 'Is there anything in the world more marvellous than the forces of Nature?'

M: 'There is.'

Q: 'And what is that?'

M: 'The power of comprehending those natural forces.'

Q: 'Is cosmic vitality the Way (Tao)?'

M: 'Cosmic vitality is cosmic vitality. The Tao is the Tao.'

Q: 'If so, they must be two different things?'

M: 'That which knows does not proceed from two different persons.'

Q: 'What is wrong and what is right?'

M: 'Wrong is the mind that attends to externals; right is the mind that brings externals under control.'

* * *

7. A Vinaya Master named Yüan once came and asked: 'Do you make efforts in your practice of the Way, Master?'

M: 'Yes, I do.'

Q: 'How?'

M: 'When hungry, I eat; when tired, I sleep.'

Q: 'And does everybody make the same efforts as you do, Master?'

M: 'Not in the same way.'

Q: 'Why not?'

M: 'When they are eating, they think of a hundred kinds

of necessities, and when they are going to sleep they ponder over affairs of a thousand different kinds. That is how they differ from me.'[95]

At this, the Vinaya Master was silenced.

*   *   *

8. The Venerable Yün Kuang once asked: 'Master, do you know where you will be reborn?'

M: 'We have not died yet; so what is the use of discussing our rebirths? That which knows birth is the unborn. We cannot stray from birth to speak of the unborn. The Patriarch once said: "That which undergoes birth is really unborn." '[96]

Q: 'Does this apply even to those who have yet to perceive their own nature?'

M: 'Your not having perceived your own nature does not imply that you lack that nature. Why so? Because perception itself is that nature; without it, we should never be able to perceive anything. Consciousness is also that nature, whence it is called the nature of Consciousness. Understanding is also that nature, whence it is called the nature of Understanding. That which can produce the myriad phenomena (dharmas) of the universe is called the Dharma Nature, otherwise known as the Dharmakāya. The Patriarch Aśvaghoṣa[97] declared: "In speaking of phenomena (dharmas), we really refer to the minds of sentient beings; for, when mental processes (literally 'mindings', hsin) occur, all sorts of phenomena take birth in accordance with them; and, when mental processes do not occur, phenomena have nothing in which to arise—there are not even names for them." Deluded people, who do not know that the Dharmakāya is immaterial but becomes manifest in response to the needs of men,[98] may say that "fresh bamboos are the Dharmakāya" and that "luxuriant clusters of yellow flowers are nothing but Prajñā"! Yet, if flowers are Prajñā, then Prajñā must be identical with non-sentient matter; and, if green bamboos are the Dharmakāya, then the Dharmakāya is a vegetable, so that people dining off bamboo shoots are actually EATING the Dharmakāya![99] Is this sort of talk worth recording? Instead of recognizing the Buddha right in front of you, you spend aeon after aeon searching for him. His whole substance pervades all phenomena, but you are deluded and look for him elsewhere! Consequently, he who understands the Way (Tao) is never off it, whether he is walking, standing, sitting or lying. He who awakens to the Dharma is sovereign and at ease in all situations, since none of them are outside the Dharma.'

*   *   *

9. Presently, the Venerable Yün Kuang asked some further questions.

Q: 'Can spiritual wisdom spring from the great emptiness (t'ai hsü)? Is real mind the causal product of good and evil? Can those indulging their desires be on the Way? Can those clinging to right and wrong develop unimpeded use of mind? Can those in whom sense-impressions stir up mental processes achieve one-pointed concentration (ting)? Do people who remain constantly in motionless abstraction really possess wisdom? Do those who treat others with contempt really possess egos? Are those grasping at "is" and "is not" really wise? Men who seek realization through book-knowledge,[100] men who seek the Buddha by means of austerities, men who stray from their minds in quest of

G

Buddhahood and men who cling to mind's being the Buddha—are all these various people acting in accord with the Way? I beg you, Master, to reply to these points one by one.'

M: 'The great emptiness does not give birth to spiritual wisdom. Real mind is not the causal product of good and evil. Men whose evil desires lie deep have exceedingly shallow potentials. The minds of those clinging to right and wrong are obstructed. Those in whom sense-impressions stir up mental processes seldom achieve one-pointed concentration. In those who remain constantly in a state of motionless abstraction, forgetful of the mysterious source of that stillness, wisdom is at a low ebb. Self-importance and contempt for others intensify the illusion of an ego. Those grasping at "is" and "is not" are stupid. Those who seek realization in book-knowledge pile up more obstructions for themselves. Those who seek the Buddha by means of austerities are all deluded. Those who stray from their minds in quest of Buddhahood are heretics. Those who cling to mind as being the Buddha are devils!'[101]

A: 'If all that is so, ultimately, we find there is just nothing at all.'

M: 'We have come to the ultimate extent of yourself, Venerable Sir, but not to the ultimate.'

At this, the venerable monk, who was now filled with joy, hastened to prostrate himself in gratitude and departed.

*   *   *

10. Once our Master took his place in the assembly hall and said: 'It is far better for all of you to be unconcerned men.[102] Why all this craze for karmic activities that will put felons' cangues about your necks and send you down

to hell? Toiling and moiling the whole day through, telling people you are practising Ch'an and studying the Way, holding forth about your understanding of the Buddha-Dharma—this sort of thing is no use at all. It simply amounts to rushing about in pursuit of sounds and forms. Ah, when will you desist from it all? Once this poor monk heard the great Ma Tsu of Kiangsi say: "Your own treasure house contains absolutely everything you need. Use it freely instead of searching vainly for something outside yourself." From that day forward, I desisted. Making use of your own treasure house according to your needs—that can be called happiness! There is no single thing (dharma) which can be grasped or rejected. When you cease looking on things in their temporal aspect, and as having come or gone, then in the whole universe—above, below and round about—there will be no grain of anything which is not your own treasure. All you have to do is carefully to contemplate your own minds; then the marvellous trinity of Three Jewels in One Substance[103] will constantly manifest itself; of this there is no shadow of doubt. Do not search for the truth with your intellects. Do not search at all. The nature of the mind is intrinsically pure. Therefore it is written in the Avataṁsaka Sūtra:[104] "All things have no beginning; and all things have no end." Before those who are able to interpret these words correctly the Buddhas are ever present. Moreover, in the Vimalakīrti Sūtra it is written: "It is through your own bodies that Reality is perceived; the Buddha is perceived in the same manner." If you do not follow sounds and sights so that they stir your minds, and if you do not pursue appearances so that they give rise to discriminations, you will then be unconcerned men. Don't stand there for so long. Take good care of yourselves!'[105]

*　　　*　　　*

11. Upon the same day, as the assembly of monks did not break up at the usual time, the Master said: 'Why do you not disperse? This poor monk has already sat face to face with you.[106] Just go and rest.[107] What doubts do you still entertain?[108] Do not misuse your minds and waste your energy. If something is still bothering you, hurry up and ask whatever you wish.'

Then Fa Yüan, one of the monks present, asked: 'What are Buddha, Dharma and Saṅgha; what are the Three Jewels in One Substance? We beg you, Master, to explain.'

M: 'Mind is the Buddha and it is needless to use this Buddha to seek the Buddha. Mind is the Dharma and it is needless to use this Dharma to seek the Dharma. Buddha and Dharma are not separate entities and their together-ness forms the Saṅgha. Such is the meaning of Three Jewels in One Substance. A sūtra says: "Mind, Buddha and sen-tient beings—there is no difference between any of them. When your body, speech and mind are purified, we say a Buddha has appeared in the world. When these three become impure, we say a Buddha has been extinguished." For example, when you are angry you are not joyous, and when you are joyous you are not angry; yet, in both cases, there is only the one mind which is not of two substances. Fundamental wisdom is self-existent; when the passionless (anāṣraya—that which is outside the stream of trans-migration) appears, it is like a snake becoming a dragon without changing its scaly skin. Likewise, when a sentient being turns his mind towards Buddhahood, he does not change his physiognomy. Our Nature, which is intrinsically pure, does not rely on any practice in order to achieve its own state. Only the arrogant[109] claim that there are practice and realization. The real void is without obstruction and its function is, under all circumstances, inexhaustible. It is without beginning or end. A man of high spirituality is capable of sudden Illumination, whereon its function will be (seen to be) unsurpassable—this is Anuttara-samyak-sambodhi (Unexcelled Enlightenment). Mind has neither form nor shape; it is the subtle Sambhogakāya. That which is formless is the Dharmakāya of Reality. That of which the nature and phenomenal expression are void is the Boundless Immaterial Body. That which is adorned with a myriad modes of salvation is the Dharmakāya of Merit, which is the fundamental power responsible for the conversion of sentient beings; it (mind) is named according to how it appears and its wisdom is inexhaustible—hence it is called the Inexhaustible Treasury. As the progenitor of all phenomena (dharmas), it is called the Primal Dharma Treasury. As the container of all knowledge, it is called the Wisdom Treasury. As the Suchness to which all phenomena ultimately return, it is called the Tathāgata Treasury. The Diamond Sūtra says: "Tathāgata means the Suchness of all dharmas." Another sūtra says: "Of all the dharmas in the universe coming into existence and fading out of existence, there is not one which does not return to the Suchness." '

* * *

12. A guest staying at the monastery said: 'I do not know which of these three—a Vinaya Master (upholder of monastic discipline), a Dharma Master (skilled preacher) or a Ch'an Master—is the greatest. I beg you, Master, out of compassion for my ignorance, to make the matter clear to me.'

M: 'The Vinaya Masters expound the Discipline Section of the Scriptures and transmit the ancient tradition for preserving the infinite life of the Dharma (Doctrine). Seeing clearly who are the upholders and who are the transgressors of the disciplinary rules, they know how to encourage the former and to restrain the latter. They know how to comport themselves in accordance with the rules and regulations in a manner which inspires respect. They officiate at the three kinds of confession which precede transmission of the Vinaya, and they teach the initial steps leading to the four grades of sainthood. Unless they have spent their lives virtuously up to the onset of old age, how will they dare take charge of those duties? The Dharma Masters sit crosslegged upon their lion-thrones pouring forth rivers of eloquence to huge crowds, expounding means of chiselling a way through the Mysterious Pass or of opening the marvellous Gates of Prajñā by which the void-ness of giver, receiver and alms is revealed.[110] Who, unless he can trample all before him like a lion or an elephant, would dare undertake to be a match for all this? The Ch'an Masters grasp at essentials and gain a direct under-standing of the Mind Source. Their methods consist of revealing and hiding, of exposing and covering, reality in a criss-cross manner which responds adequately to all the different grades of potentiality (for Enlightenment). They excel in harmonizing facts with the underlying principle, so that people may suddenly perceive the Tathāgata; and, by pulling up their deep saṁsāric roots, they cause their pupils to experience samādhi on the spot. Thus, unless they are capable of achieving tranquillizing dhyāna and imper-turbable abstraction, they are certainly bound to be flustered under such circumstances. Although the three methods of training—discipline, dhyāna and wisdom— differ in that they present the Dharma in a manner suited to the capability of each individual, once a disciple has awakened to their profound meaning by forgetting all about the wording, how do they differ from the One Vehicle?[111] Wherefore it is written in a sūtra: "In all the Buddha-Realms of the Ten Quarters, there is only the Dharma of the One Vehicle"—there is neither a second nor a third, except in so far as the Buddha employed relative terms in his expedient teaching for the guidance of sentient beings.'

'Master,' exclaimed the guest, 'you have penetrated the Buddha-Dharma's profundity and your dialectic powers are unimpeded.'

Then he asked a further question: 'Do Confucianism, Taoism and Buddhism really amount to one doctrine or to three?'

M: 'Employed by men of great capacity, they are the same. As understood by men of limited intellect, they differ. All of them spring forth from the functioning of the one self-nature. It is views involving differentiation which make them three. Whether a man remains deluded or gains Illumination depends upon himself, not upon differences or similarity of doctrine.'

*   *   *

13. The Venerable Tao Kuang, who was an adherent of the Dharmalakṣaṇa School (which holds that consciousness is real) and also a commentator upon the Scriptures, enquired: 'Master, what mental processes (hsin) do you employ in pursuing the Way?'

M: 'I have no mental processes that would be of use and no Way to follow.'

Q: 'If both those statements are true, why is it that every day you convene gatherings during which you urge others to learn how to follow the Way by means of Ch'an?'

M: 'This old monk does not possess even a dot of ground in which to stick an awl,[112] so how can he gather people? He does not have so much as a tongue,[113] then how can he urge people to do anything?'

A: 'Why, Master, you are lying to my face.'

M: 'How can this old monk, being without a tongue to urge people, tell a lie?'

A: 'Really I do not understand the way the Venerable Ch'an Master talks.'

M: 'Nor does this old monk understand himself.'[114]

*   *   *

14. The Venerable Chih, who used to expound the Avataṁsaka Sūtra, asked: 'Why will you not allow that fresh green bamboos are the Dharmakāya and that luxuriant clusters of yellow flowers are nothing but Prajñā?'

M: 'The Dharmakāya is immaterial but avails itself of the prevailing green bamboos to reveal itself. Prajñā does not differentiate[115] but avails itself of the prevailing yellow flowers to manifest itself. These yellow flowers and bamboos do not of themselves possess Prajñā or the Dharmakāya. Therefore it is written in a sūtra: "The real Dharmakāya of the Buddhas is likened to a void; it reveals itself in response to the needs of living beings like the moon being reflected in the water." If yellow flowers were Prajñā, then Prajñā would be identical with inanimate objects; if green bamboos were the Dharmakāya, then they would be capable of the Dharmakāya's responsive functioning. Do you understand, Venerable Sir?'

A: 'No, I do not.'

M: 'One who has perceived his own nature will be right whether he says that those things are Prajñā and the

Dharmakāya or that they are not; for he will carry out its function according to prevailing circumstances, without being hindered by the dual conception of right and wrong. As for someone who has not yet perceived his own nature, when he speaks of green bamboos, he forms a rigid concept of green bamboos as such; and, when he speaks of yellow flowers, he forms the same sort of rigid concept. Moreover, when he speaks of the Dharmakāya, it becomes an obstruction to him, and he talks of Prajñā without knowing what it is. Thus, everything he says remains at the level of theoretical debate.'

Chih bowed his thanks and withdrew.

*   *   *

15. Somebody once asked: 'How much time do we need to attain deliverance by setting our minds on practising the Dharma?'

M: 'Using the mind for practices is like washing dirty things in sticky mud. Prajñā is mysterious and wonderful. Itself unbegotten, its mighty functioning is at our service regardless of times and seasons.'

Q: 'Can ordinary people succeed in mastering those functions?'

M: 'Those who have perceived their own nature are no longer ordinary people. The Supreme Vehicle of Sudden Illumination transcends ordinary and holy alike. While deluded people are talking of ordinary and holy, Illumined men leap over Saṁsāra and Nirvāṇa—both! While deluded people are speaking of facts and of the underlying principle, Illumined men exercise their function without restriction. While deluded people seek achievement and realization, Illumined men remain free from both. While

deluded people set their hopes upon some far-distant aeon,
Illumined men instantly perceive all.'

*   *   *

16. Once a commentator on the Vimalakīrti Sūtra said:
'It is written in our sūtra: "You should regard the six
heretics as your teachers. After you have joined the Order,
you should be misled by them and take part in their fall.
Those giving you alms should not be called cultivators of
the field of blessedness. Those making you offerings should
fall into the three evil states of existence. You should vilify
the Buddha and destroy the Dharma. You should not
belong to the Saṅgha and you should not attain deliverance.[116] If you can behave like this, you may take my
food." I ask you, Master, to give me a clear explanation of
this passage.'

M: 'The six teachers is a term for the six senses from
which your delusions arise. The term heretic refers to
seeking the Buddha apart from mind. Whatever can be
given away cannot be called a field of blessedness. Your
being stirred by the thought of receiving offerings will land
you amidst the three evil states.[117] If you dare to vilify the
Buddha, you are not attached to Buddha-seeking: if you
dare to slander the Dharma, you are not attached to
Dharma-seeking; and your not joining the Saṅgha implies
that you are not attached to Saṅgha-seeking. Your not
attaining deliverance means that your inherent wisdom,
now freed from this last obstruction, can manifest itself instantaneously. If you can interpret the passage in this way,
you will receive as food joy in the Dharma and the happiness of meditation (ch'an).'[118]

*   *   *

17. A man who practised meditation once asked: 'There are some who, when questioned about the Buddha, just answer: "Buddha!" Questioned about the Dharma, they simply answer: "Dharma!" This is called the one-word method. I do not know if it is right or not.'

M: 'Like parrots mimicking human speech, those people have nothing to say for themselves because they lack wisdom. Their method is similar to that of using water to cleanse water or fire to burn fire—all are absolutely valueless!'

*   *   *

18. Someone asked if words and speech are the same.[119]

M: 'The same. Speech means words arranged in sentences. Fluent dialectic resembling an ever-flowing stream, so manifold and sublime as to suggest a vessel pouring forth pearls; such is speech—it clears away the myriad phenomenal appearances, gushes forth in unending torrents of eloquence and skilfully interprets an ocean of meanings. As for words, a single syllable reveals the mind,[120] which is inwardly mysterious and profound, while outwardly it exhibits marvellous aspects; amidst a myriad disturbing forces, it remains imperturbable; and it remains for ever distinct amidst a medley of pure and impure. All this may be likened to the minister's words which made the Prince of Chi blush,[121] or to Vimalakīrti's silent preaching which Mañjuśrī praised[122]—how can ordinary men of today hope to understand such things?'

*   *   *

19. The Vinaya Master Yüan once said: 'You Ch'an Masters always claim extravagantly that Mind is the Buddha. You are wrong, for even Bodhisattvas at the first

stage[123] (of development into Buddhas) can appear in bodily forms in a hundred different Buddha-Realms, and those at the second stage can multiply themselves ten times more than that. (Since Mind is the Buddha), will the Ch'an Master try out his miraculous powers and do the same for me to see?'

M: 'Venerable Achārya, are you yourself an ordinary or a saintly monk?'

A: 'Ordinary.'

M: 'Since you are but an ordinary monk, how can you ask questions about matters like that? This is what a sūtra means by saying: "The Virtuous One's mind is turned upside down and does not accord with the Buddha-Wisdom." '[124]

A: 'You Ch'an Masters always say that if we awaken to the Way right in front of us, we shall attain deliverance in our present bodily form. You are wrong.'

M: 'Suppose a man, after a lifetime of virtuous conduct, suddenly puts forth his hand and steals something. Is that person a thief in his present bodily form?'

A: 'Obviously, yes.'

M: 'Then, if at this moment someone suddenly perceives his own nature, tell me why he cannot be delivered?'

A: 'At this moment? Impossible! According to the sūtras, three aeons-of-uncountable-extent (asamkhyeya-kalpas) must pass before we attain to it.'[125]

M: 'Can aeons-of-uncountable-extent be counted?'

At this Yüan shouted indignantly: 'Can someone who draws an analogy between thievery and liberation claim that he reasons correctly?'

M: 'Achārya, you do not understand the Way, but you should not prevent others from understanding it. Your own eyes are shut, so you get angry when others see.'

Red in the face, Yüan began striding away, but called over his shoulder: 'Who's an old muddlehead right off the Way?'

M: 'That which is striding away is just your Way.'[126]

*　　　*　　　*

20. A venerable monk called Hui, who preached the Chih-Kuan doctrine (of the T'ien T'ai School), asked: 'Master, are you able to discern demons?'

M: 'Yes. A stirred mind is the heavenly demon; a stirless mind is the demon of the five aggregates;[127] a mind that is sometimes stirred and sometimes stirless is the passion (kleśa) demon. According to this "right" dharma of mine, there should be none of these.'

Q: 'What is the meaning of (the T'ien T'ai practice of) simultaneous meditation upon the One Mind's three aspects?'[128]

M: 'Besides the past mind which is already gone, the future mind which has yet to come, and the present mind which does not stay, which mind will you use for your meditation?'

A: 'So the Venerable Ch'an Master does not understand the Chih-Kuan teaching (to which I alluded).'

M: 'Do you understand it, Venerable Commentator?'

A: 'I do.'

M: 'As the great Master Chih Chê[129] said: "Chih (silencing the mind to obtain samādhi) is preached to wipe out (the illusion of) Chih; and Kuan (looking into the mind to cause Prajñā to appear and function normally) is preached to eradicate the illusion of Kuan. To dwell on Chih is to drown oneself in the ocean of birth and death; to abide in Kuan is to upset the mind." Will you use the mind to put a stop to mind and stir the mind to meditate on it? Setting the mind on meditation involves attachment to permanence; setting no mind on meditation involves annihilation. Clinging to the concept of "either existence or non-existence" implies (attachment to) a dualism.[130] Then how will the Venerable Commentator expound (the Chih-Kuan practice) correctly for me to see?'

A: 'Since you put it like that, there is really nothing I can say.'

M: 'If so, have you ever really understood the Chih-Kuan practice?'

*   *   *

21. Someone asked: 'Is Prajñā very large?'

M: 'It is.'

Q: 'How large?'

M: 'Unlimited.'

Q: 'Is Prajñā small?'

M: 'It is.'

Q: 'How small?'

M: 'So small as to be invisible.'

Q: 'Where is it?'

M: 'Where is it not?'[131]

*   *   *

22. A monk commentator of the Vimalakīrti Nirdeśa Sūtra enquired: 'According to our sūtra: "After all the Bodhisattvas who were present had spoken of their interpretation of the non-dual Dharma-Gate (to Enlightenment), Vimalakīrti remained silent." Is that the ultimate?'[132]

M: 'It is not. If the sacred meaning had been wholly

revealed (by that), there would have been nothing more for the third section of the sūtra to say.'

After a long pause, the commentator enquired: 'Will the Venerable Ch'an Master explain to me the ultimate meaning that was not wholly revealed.'

M: 'The first section of that sūtra taught the Buddha's ten chief disciples how their minds should abide. The second section described how each of the Bodhisattvas present spoke of his entry into the non-dual Dharma-gate; they used words to reveal that which is wordless. Mañjuśrī, however, revealed the wordless through absence of words and speech; whereas Vimalakīrti employed neither words nor absence of words to wind up their statements. The third section began after Vimalakīrti's silence and went on to reveal the transcendental function. Does the Venerable Commentator understand?'

A: 'Well, what a strange way of putting it!'

M: 'It is not so strange.'

Q: 'Why not?'

M: 'I explain it like that to wipe out passionate clinging to the reality of an ego. If you take the sūtra's real meaning, it tells you only that the material and immaterial are void and still (i.e. in the Nirvāṇic condition), so as to enable you to perceive your own nature. It teaches you how to give up wrong practices in favour of right practice. So you must not allow your mind to give rise to discriminative thoughts about words, speech and printed texts. It would be quite enough if you could fully understand just the two words composing Vimalakīrti's name. Vimala (Spotless) refers to the fundamental "substance" and Kīrti (Reputation) is its functional manifestation.[133] This functional manifestation proceeds from the fundamental "substance" and it is by means of it that we return to that "substance".

Since "substance" and manifestation are One in reality, the fundamental and its manifestation do not differ from each other.[134] For this reason the ancients said: "Though the fundamental and its manifestations are different denominations, the Inconceivable (of which they are aspects) is but One; and yet, even that One is not one."[135] Had you understood the real meaning of the two denominations expediently termed Vimala (Spotless) and Kīrti (Reputation), it would be superfluous to speak of the ultimate and the not-ultimate. (There is only that which is) neither preliminary nor final, neither root nor twig and neither vimala nor kīrti. The instruction consists in revealing to sentient beings their fundamental nature which cognizes its own indescribable state of deliverance. Those who have not perceived their own nature will never in all their lives understand this doctrine.'

*   *   *

23. A monk asked: 'Since all the myriad phenomena (dharmas) are non-existent, the nature of mind should also be non-existent. Just as a bubble having burst can never reform, so can a man once dead never be reborn, for nothing remains of him. Where will the nature of his mind be then?'

M: 'Bubbles are composed of water. When a bubble bursts, does the water composing it cease to be? Our bodies proceed from our real nature. When we die, why should you say that our nature is no more?'

A: 'If you maintain there is such a nature, bring it forth and show it to me!'

M: 'Do you believe there will be a morrow?'

A: 'Yes, certainly.'

M: 'Bring it forth and show it to me!'

A: 'There will surely be a morrow, but not just now.'

M: 'Yes, but its not being just now does not mean that there will be no morrow. You personally do not perceive your own nature, but this does not mean that your nature does not exist. Just now, there is before you that which wears a robe, takes food and walks, stands, sits or reclines, but you do not recognize it (for what it is). You may well be called a stupid and deluded person. If you discriminate between today and tomorrow, that is like using your own nature to search for your own nature; you will not perceive it even after myriads of aeons.[136] Yours is a case of not seeing the sun, not of there being no sun.'

*   *   *

24. A monk who used to give lectures on the Ch'ing Lung (Green Dragon) Commentary[137] (on the Diamond Sūtra) enquired: 'Our sūtra says: "(When the Tathāgata expounds the Dharma) there is really no Dharma to teach; but this is (expediently) called teaching the Dharma." How does the Venerable Ch'an Master interpret this passage?'

M: 'The substance of Prajñā is utterly pure and does not contain a single thing on which to lay hold—this is the meaning of "there is no Dharma to teach". As this nirvāṇic substance, Prajñā, is endowed with functions countless as the sands of the Ganges, there is not a thing which can escape its knowledge—this is the meaning of "this is (expediently) called preaching the Dharma".'

*   *   *

H

25. A commentator of the Avataṁsaka Sūtra asked: 'Do you believe that inanimate objects are Buddhas?'

M: 'I do not. If inanimate objects were Buddhas, then a living man would be inferior to a dead man; why, even dead donkeys and dead dogs ought to be superior to him! A sūtra says: "The Buddha-Body is the Dharmakāya; it is begotten of discipline, dhyāna and wisdom, by the three insights, the six transcendental powers[138] and by the performance of all excellent modes of salvation." If an inanimate object were the Buddha, then, were Your Reverence to die now, you would automatically become a Buddha!'

*   *   *

26. A Dharma Master enquired: 'Do you believe that the greatest merit derives from the recitation of the Prajñā Sūtra?'

M: 'I do not.'

Q: 'So all ten volumes of the *Stories of Divine Responses*[139] are unworthy of belief?'

M: 'Filial piety practised while parents are still alive ensures divine responses (and rewards); this does not mean you have to wait until after their death so that their bleached skeletons may bless you.[140] Sūtras are made of paper covered with words printed in ink, but printed words, paper and ink are without self-nature; so from whence will those divine responses capable of fulfilling your wishes come? Effectual answers come from proper use of the mind by the person who reads the sūtras; and this explains how the divine power works in response to appeal from a living being. You may test this for yourself by taking a volume of the sūtras and leaving it quietly on a table. If nobody picks it up and recites it and practises it, do you suppose it can possibly have any marvellous efficacy in itself?'

*   *   *

27. A monk enquired: 'How are we to interpret correctly all names, forms, speech and silence in order to integrate them and realize a state that is neither anterior nor posterior?'[141]

M: 'When a thought arises, fundamentally there is neither form nor name; how can you speak in terms of before and after? Failure to understand the essential purity of all that has name and form is the cause of your mistakenly reckoning everything in those terms. People are locked in by these names and forms, and, lacking the key of wisdom, they are unable to unlock themselves. Those clinging to the Middle Way suffer from Middle Way psychosis; those grasping at extremes suffer from a dualist psychosis. You do not comprehend that that which manifests itself right now is the unequalled Dharmakāya.[142] Delusion and awakening, as well as gain and loss, pertain to the worldly way. The rising (of the thought) of creation and destruction leads to the burial of true wisdom; both the cutting off of defilements (kleśa) and the search for Bodhi are in direct opposition to wisdom.'

*   *   *

28. Once somebody asked: 'Why do the Vinaya Masters not believe in Ch'an?'
M: 'The Noumenon is profoundly mysterious and not easily revealed, whereas names and forms are easy to grasp. Those who do not perceive their self-nature refuse to

believe in it; those who do perceive their self-nature are called Buddhas. Only those who recognize the Buddha can believe in and enter the Noumenon. The Buddha does not flee from men; it is men who flee the Buddha. Buddhahood can be realized only by the mind. While deluded men seek it through printed words, Illumined men look into their minds and realize Bodhi. Deluded men sow causal deeds and await their fruition, whereas Illumined men understand the immateriality of mind. Deluded men cling to the (illusory) ego and hold it to be their very own, but Illumined men employ their Prajñā which, when called upon to do so, manifests itself instantaneously. Deluded men are hindered by their clinging to "is" and "is not", while men of wisdom perceive their own nature and understand the marvellous interpenetration of all forms. Those who have reached only the "dry wisdom"[143] stage grow weary of their dialectics, whereas men of (real) wisdom and clear understanding set their minds at rest. When a Bodhisattva touches anything (his wisdom) shines upon it (enabling him to perceive it as it really is), while a śrāvaka darkens his mind with fear of his surroundings.[144] Illumined men, in their daily activities, do not stray from the Uncreate, but deluded men screen themselves from the Buddha who is right in front of them.'

*　　　　*　　　　*

29. Once somebody asked: 'How can we obtain the power of bodily freedom from natural law?'

M: 'Spiritual self-nature pervades all worlds which are countless as the sands of the Ganges; it penetrates mountains, rivers, rocks and cliffs without hindrance, leaping an infinite distance in a single moment, going and coming

without trace. Fire cannot burn it, nor water drown it.
Fools, having no mind-wisdom, want their (bodies which
are composed of the) four elements to fly! It is written in a
sūtra that ordinary people who cling to forms must be
taught in accordance with their capacities. So mind's
formlessness is described as the subtle Sambhogakāya.[145]
That which is immaterial is Reality, the "substance" of
which is void; hence it is called the Boundless Space-like
Body. As it is adorned with merits deriving from a myriad
modes of salvation, it is called the Dharmakāya of Merit,
the source of all befitting activities. Despite all these names
derived from its varied functions, in reality there is but the
pure Dharmakāya.'

*　　　*　　　*

30. Somebody once asked: 'If we follow the Way with undivided mind, will the load of karmic obstructions resulting
from our past deeds be dissipated?'

M: 'For those who have not yet perceived their own
nature, it will not be dissipated; whereas those who perceive it thereby wipe out all karmic obstruction just as the
hot sun melts the frost and snow. They may be likened to
people able to burn up all the grass covering the mighty
slopes of Mount Sumeru in a single flash, for their karmic
obstruction is like that grass and their wisdom is like that
fire!'

Q: 'How can we know when all karmic obstructions have
been dissipated?'

M: 'When you see through to the mind now manifesting
itself in front of you, all arising concepts of past and present
will be viewed in the light of that perception. All past and
future Buddhas, together with the myriad phenomena, will

be seen as appearing simultaneously. The sūtra says: "Knowledge of all phenomena contained in a single thought-moment is a Bodhimaṇḍala, for it ensures achievement of (the Buddha's) universal knowledge (sarvajña)." '

*　　*　　*

31. A man who practised meditation once asked: 'How can I abide in the right dharma?'

M: 'To seek abode in the RIGHT dharma is WRONG. Why so? Because the "right" dharma is neither wrong nor right.'

Q: 'Then how am I to become a Buddha?'

M: 'You need not cast aside the worldly mind; just refrain from soiling your self-nature. The sūtra says: "Mind, Buddha and living beings do not differ from one another." '

Q: 'Can we gain deliverance just by interpreting in this way?'

M: 'Since fundamentally you are not bound, why seek deliverance? The Dharma is beyond mere words, speech and writings. Do not seek it amidst a plethora of sentences. The Dharma does not pertain to past, present and future; you cannot unite with it at the level of causal law. The Dharma transcends everything and is incomparable. The Dharmakāya, though immaterial, manifests itself in response to the needs of living beings; so you cannot turn away from the worldly to seek deliverance.'

*　　*　　*

32. A monk enquired the meaning of Prajñā.

M: 'If you suppose that anything is NOT Prajñā, let me hear what it is?'

Q: 'How may we perceive our own nature?'

M: 'That which perceives is your own nature; without it there could be no perception.'

Q: 'Then what is self-cultivation?'

M: 'Refraining from befouling your own nature and from deceiving yourself is (the practice of) self-cultivation. When your own nature's mighty function manifests itself, this is the unequalled Dharmakāya.'

Q: 'Does our own nature include evil?'

M: 'It does not even include good!'

Q: 'If it contains neither good nor evil, where should we direct it when using it?'

M: 'To set your mind on USING it is a great error.'

Q: 'Then what should we do to be right?'

M: 'There is nothing to do and nothing which can be called right.'[146]

*　　　*　　　*

33. Once somebody enquired: 'Suppose a man is sitting in a boat and the boat-keel cuts to death a shell-fish. Is the man guilty or should the boat be blamed?'

M: 'Man and boat had no mind to kill the shell-fish, and the only person to be blamed is you.[147] When a tearing wind snaps off a branch which falls and kills somebody, there is no murderer and no murdered. In all the world, there is no place where living beings do not have to suffer.'

*　　　*　　　*

34. A monk asked: 'I still do not understand how realization can be achieved in a single thought-moment (kṣaṇa) by relying on (someone's) displaying certain feelings or passions, or on his pointing at the surrounding objects,

his speech or silence, his raising his eyebrows or moving his eyes.'[148]

M: 'There is nothing which is outside self-nature. Its function is marvellous—marvellous in its motion and in its stillness. One who has (attained to) real mind expresses that reality whether he speaks or keeps silent. For one who understands the Way, walking, standing, sitting or lying— all are the Way. When the self-nature is obscured by delusion, a myriad illusions arise.'

Q: 'What is the meaning of "a dharma (doctrine) has its aims"?'

M: 'From the moment of its establishment, a dharma (doctrine) is complete in all its meanings. (As the sūtra says:) "Mañjuśrī, all dharmas (doctrines) are established upon basic impermanence." '[149]

Q: 'Do you mean that there is just a great emptiness?'

M: 'Are you scared by emptiness?'[150]

A: 'Yes, I am scared.'

M: 'That which is scared is not the same as a great emptiness.'

Q: 'How shall we understand that which is beyond the reach of words?'

M: 'Now, while you are speaking, what is there which cannot be reached by your words?'[151]

*   *   *

35. There were over ten older monks who came and asked the Master: 'There is a sūtra which speaks of the destruction of the Buddha-Dharma, but we do not know if the Buddha-Dharma is destructible.'

M: 'Worldlings and heretics claim that it can be destroyed, whereas śrāvakas and pratyeka-Buddhas hold it to be indestructible. The "right" dharma of mine has no room for these two opinions. As to that "right" dharma, it is not only worldlings and heretics who have not yet reached the Buddha-stage, for the followers of the two smaller vehicles (śrāvakas and pratyeka-Buddhas) are just as bad.'

Q: 'Do the dharmas (doctrines) that treat of reality, illusion, immateriality and materiality each have a seed-nature.'[152]

M: 'Although a dharma itself has no seed-nature, it manifests itself in response to the needs of living beings. When the mind abides in illusion, everything becomes illusory; if there were a single dharma (phenomenon) not illusory, illusion would be stable! If the mind is immaterial, everything is immaterial; if there were a single dharma not immaterial, the concept of immateriality would not be valid. When you are deluded, you run after a dharma; when you are enlightened, you can manipulate it! The utmost limit of the universe with all its immense variety is space; and all earth's many rivers merge with their final destination, the sea; all saints and sages can reach their apotheosis in Buddhahood; and the twelve divisions of the canon, the five groupings of Vinaya and the five groupings of śāstras have for their highest aim realization of own-mind. Mind is the marvellous basis of Dhāraṇī[153] and the great source of all phenomena; it is called the Storehouse of Great Wisdom or the Non-Abiding Nirvāṇa.[154] Although there are innumerable names for it, all serve to designate Mind.'

Q: 'What is illusion?'

M: 'Illusion has no stable appearance; it is like a whirling fire,[155] like a mirage city, like puppets on strings, like (the mirage oases caused by) sunbeams, like flowers in the sky—none are real.'

Q: 'Who is the great illusionist?'

A: 'Mind is the great illusionist; the body is the city of great illusion, and names are its garments and sustenance. In all the worlds, countless as Ganges sands, there is not anything which is outside illusion. Worldlings, unable to understand illusion, are deluded by illusory karma wherever they happen to be. Śrāvakas, being afraid of illusory phenomena, darken their minds and enter a state of stillness (i.e. relative Nirvāṇa). Bodhisattvas, knowing all illusions and understanding that their substance is illusory, are indifferent to all names and forms. The Buddha is the great illusionist who turned the great illusory Dharma-Wheel, attained illusory Nirvāṇa, transmuted illusory saṁsāra into that which is beyond birth and death, and transformed lands of filth, innumerable as the sands of the Ganges, into the pure Dharma-Dhātu.'

*   *   *

36. A monk once enquired: 'Why do you forbid people to intone the sūtras and liken intoning them to speaking in a foreign language?'

M: 'Because such people are like parrots mimicking human speech without understanding its meaning. The sūtras transmit the Buddha's meaning, and those who intone them without understanding that meaning are merely imitating someone else's words. That is why I do not allow it.'

Q: 'Can there be any meaning apart from writings, words and speech?'

M: 'Your talking like that reveals that you are just an imitator of other people's words.'

Q: 'We, too, are now using words. Why are you so dead set against their use?'[156]

M: 'Now, listen attentively. Sūtras are writings set forth in specific order. When I speak, I use meaningful words which are not writings. When (most) living beings speak, they employ words from writings, but they are not meaningful. To comprehend (real) meanings, we should go beyond unsteady words; to awaken to the fundamental law, we should leap beyond writings. The Dharma is beyond words, speech and writings; how can it be sought amid a plethora of sentences? That is why those seeking enlightenment forget all about wording after having arrived at the (real) meaning. Awakened to reality, they throw away the doctrine just as a fisherman, having caught his fish, pays no more attention to his nets; or as a hunter, after catching his rabbit, forgets about his snare.'

*   *   *

37. A Dharma Master asked: 'Master, what do you think about the statement that constant repetition of the Buddha's name is a form of Mahāyāna involving realism?'

M: 'Even idealism is not Mahāyānist, how much less so realism! A sūtra says: "Ordinary people who cleave to forms must be taught according to their capacities." '

Q: 'As to the vow to be born in the Pure Land, is there really a Pure Land?'

M: 'A sūtra says: "Those who wish to attain the Pure Land should purify their minds and then their pure minds ARE the Pure Land of the Buddha." If your mind is pure and clean, you will find the Pure Land wherever you happen to be. By way of illustration—an heir born to a prince is destined to succeed to the throne; likewise, he who sets his mind on the quest for Buddhahood will be born into the

Buddha's Pure Land. He whose mind is corrupt will be born in a land of filth. Purity and corruption depend solely on the mind, not on the land.'

Q: 'I am always hearing talk of the Way (Tao, here meaning self-nature), but I do not know who can perceive it.'

M: 'Those possessing the Wisdom-Eye can perceive it.'

Q: 'I am very fond of the Mahāyāna, but how shall I study it with success?'

M: 'He who awakens (to mind) can achieve success; he who is not awakened to it cannot.'

Q: 'What shall I do to be awakened to it?'

M: 'It comes only by true intuition.'

Q: 'What is it like?'

M: 'It resembles nothing.'

Q: 'If so, it should be ultimately non-existent.'

M: 'That which is non-existent is not ultimate.'

Q: 'Then it must exist.'

M: 'It does exist, but it is formless.'

Q: 'If I do not awaken to it, what shall I do?'

M: 'It is of your own accord that Your Reverence fails to awaken to it; nobody is preventing you.'

Q: 'Does the Buddha-Dharma appertain to time?'

M: 'It is to be perceived in the formless, so it is not external; but nor, with its infinite powers of responding to circumstances, is it internal; and, as there is nowhere between them where it abides, it cannot be grasped on the time-level.'

A: 'This way of talking is much too confusing.'

M: 'Just now, when you used the word "confusing", was there anything internal or external about it?'[157]

A: 'I cannot search, then, for any trace of it within or without.'

M: 'If (you understand) there is no trace, it is clear that what I said just now was not confusing.'[158]

Q: 'What shall we do to attain Buddhahood?'

M: 'This mind is (fundamentally) the Buddha and can become a Buddha (in actuality).'[159]

Q: 'When beings enter hell, does their Buddha-Nature accompany them?'

M: 'When you are actually engaged in doing evil, is there any good in that action?'

A: 'No, there is not.'

M: 'When beings enter hell, the Buddha-Nature is similarly (not present).'[160]

Q: 'But how is it then with the Buddha-Nature which every being possesses?'

M: 'If you perform the Buddha's function, that is employing the Buddha-Nature. If you steal, that is employing the nature of a thief. If you behave in the worldly way, that is employing the nature of (ordinary) living beings. This nature, being formless and without characteristics, is variously named in accordance with the ways in which it functions. The Diamond Sūtra says: "All the virtuous ones (bhadra) and enlightened saints (ārya) are distinguished by (their conformity with) the non-active dharma (anās-rava, wu wei)." '

*   *   *

38. A monk once asked: 'What is the Buddha?'

M: 'There is no Buddha apart from mind.'

Q: 'What is the Dharmakāya?'

M: 'Mind is the Dharmakāya. As it is the source of all the myriad phenomena, we refer to it as the Body of the Dharma Realm. The Śāstra of the Awakening of Faith says: "In speaking of the Dharma, we refer to the mind of sentient beings, for our revelations of the Mahāyāna truths all depend on Mind." '

Q: 'What is meant by saying that the Great Sūtra[161] resides in a small particle of dust?'

M: 'Wisdom is that sūtra. A sūtra says: "There is a great sūtra (book) with a capacity equal to that of a major-chiliocosm (tri-sahasra-mahā-sahasra-loka-dhātu) which yet resides in a small particle of dust." By a particle of dust is meant the mind-dust giving rise to a single thought. Therefore it is said: "In a thought stirred by mind-dust, there are elaborated as many gāthās as there are sands in the Ganges." Today people no longer understand this.'

Q: 'What is the City of Great Meaning and who is the King of Great Meaning?'

M: 'The body is that city and mind is that king. A sūtra says: "Those who listen much are skilled in truth, but not in putting it into words." Words are transient, but meaning is eternal, for it is without form and characteristics. Apart from words and speech, there is Mind which is the Great Sūtra (book). Mind is the King of Great Meaning; he who does not clearly know his mind is not a skilful (interpreter) of the meaning; he is just an imitator of words spoken by others.'

Q: 'The Diamond Sūtra speaks of leading all the nine classes of sentient beings into the state of Final Nirvāṇa. It also says: "There are really no sentient beings to be led across." How can these two passages of Scripture be reconciled? It first says and then repeats that sentient beings really are led across, but without being attached to their forms. I have often doubted this and am still not convinced, so I beg you, Master, to explain it to me.'

M: 'These nine classes of beings are all (latent) in our

physical body; they are created according to our karmic deeds. Thus, ignorance creates a being born from an egg; defilement (kleśa) creates a being born from the womb; immersion in the love-fluid creates a being born from humidity; and the sudden arising of passion creates a being born of transformation. When awakened, we are Buddhas; when deluded, we are (ordinary) sentient beings. To a Bodhisattva, every thought arising in the mind is a living being. If every thought is looked into clearly, the substance of the mind is found to be void, and this is called the deliverance of living beings. The Illuminated man liberates his inner living beings even before they take shape in his own self; and, since their shapes therefore do not exist, it is clear that there are in reality no living beings to be liberated.'

*   *   *

39. A monk asked: 'Are words and speech also mind?'

M: 'Words and speech are concurrent causes; they are not mind.'

Q: 'What is this mind which lies beyond all concurrent causes?'

M: 'There is no mind beyond words and speech.'

Q: 'If there is no mind beyond words and speech, what is that mind in reality?'

M: 'Mind is without form and characteristics; it is neither beyond nor not beyond words and speech; it is for ever clear and still and can perform its function freely and without hindrance. The Patriarch[162] said:

It is only when the mind is seen to be unreal
That the Dharma of all minds can be truly understood.

*   *   *

40. A monk asked: What is meant by "the study of dhyāna (meditation) and wisdom (prajñā) in equal proportions"?'

M: 'Dhyāna pertains to substance and wisdom is its function. Dhyāna begets wisdom and wisdom leads to dhyāna. They may be likened to the water and its waves, both of which are of one substance with neither taking precedence over the other. Such is the study of dhyāna and wisdom in equal proportions. Homeless ones (monks) should not look to words and speech. Walking, standing, sitting and lying—all are the functioning of your nature. In what are you out of accord with it? Just go now and take a rest (i.e. set your minds at rest) for a while. As long as you are not carried away by external winds, your nature will remain like water for ever still and clear. Let nothing matter. Take good care of yourselves!'[163]

TRANSLATOR'S NOTES

[1] The zenith, nadir and eight compass points.

[2] Deliverance from Saṃsāra, the round of endless births and deaths, by entrance into Nirvāṇa. However, the higher Mahāyāna teaching, as will be seen from this book, indicates that Nirvāṇa and Saṃsāra are one and that the Illumined man sees them thus.

[3] The Chinese words are 'tun wu', of which the former means 'sudden' and the latter is identical with the Japanese word 'satori'.

[4] Deluded thoughts are thoughts involving the dualism of opposites such as love and hatred, distinctions between self and other, and all the countless thinking processes which proceed from unillumined minds.

[5] The Pure Land (Sukhāvatī) is the immediate goal of countless Chinese, Japanese, Korean and Vietnamese Buddhists, who conceive of it as a Buddha-Land formed as a result of Amida Buddha's compassionate vow to save all sentient beings who put their faith in him. In that land, beings not yet ready for Nirvāṇa are prepared by the Buddha for that ultimate stage. There are other Buddhists for whom the Pure Land is a symbol of the Dharmakāya, of purified mind and so on. Though some Western Buddhists have written scornfully of the Pure Land form of Buddhism, there is ample evidence that its methods often lead to Illumination. The symbols it employs stand for the same truths as those taught by the Zen School and offer an easier approach for certain kinds of people. The constant repetition of Amida Buddha's name, accompanied by the right mental practices, is just another way of attaining full concentration and entering into samādhi. Dr D. T. Suzuki and other eminent Zen authorities have testified to this.

[6] Original nature, self-nature, own-nature (pên hsing and tzŭ hsing) all have the same meaning. The Chinese omission of such words as 'your', 'its' and so on makes it easier for the reader to keep in mind that the self-nature of all sentient beings is one and the same.

[7] The six states of mortal being or six realms are birth in the heavens, birth as asuras, as humans, as animals, as pretas, or in

the hells. All alike are temporary conditions, though of varying duration, and none of them is a proper goal for Buddhists since even the denizens of the highest heavens are in danger of being brought low again by the turning of Saṁsāra's Wheel.

[8] Saṁsāra is said to be composed of three kinds of worlds—worlds of desire, such as this one; worlds of form without desire; and worlds of formlessness.

[9] The Buddhakāya (Buddha-Body) is another term for the Dharmakāya—the undifferentiated 'Body' in which the Buddhas and all other beings are conceived of as one with the Absolute. All of us possess this 'Body' but, prior to Illumination, are not aware of it.

[10] The act of perceiving, being a function of everyone's own-nature, continues independently of there being objects to perceive.

[11] 'Wu jan' may be translated as pure, undefiled, unstained, etc. I prefer the more literal and picturesque term 'unstained', because it fits in so well with the analogy of the surface of a mirror. A mirror can reflect every kind of form and yet remain spotless, for it is entirely indifferent to what it reflects. Our minds when purified will become similarly impervious to stain. It must be added that, from a Buddhist point of view, a stain is a stain whether it results from something we call good or something we call evil.

[12] The Diamond Body is another term for the Buddhakāya—that 'Body' which symbolizes the oneness of everyone's own-nature.

[13] This means primordial ignorance, the cause of all our wanderings in Saṁsāra's round, in that it obscures from us the fact of our Buddha-Nature and leads us into the dualism of love and hatred, good and bad, existence and non-existence, and so on. Illumination means dispersal of the darkness of this ignorance.

[14] See note 10.

[15] The inner cognizer is the highest part of our consciousness —that which knows and is fully aware of everything but which does not discriminate between one thing and another.

[16] The words 't'i' and 'yung' ('substance' and 'function') are briefly defined in the list of Chinese words offering special difficulties which appears after these notes. These two words are of the greatest importance to our understanding of Ch'an (Zen). 'Substance' is often likened to a lamp and 'function' to its light. The former would

be useless unless capable of functioning by producing light; the latter would be non-existent without the former. As already explained, the meaning of 'substance' is the intangible and indefinable reality which is the true nature of everyone, and 'function' denotes its infinite capacity to produce every sort of energy, form and so on.

[17] As will be seen from what follows, 'total abstention from action' is a phrase not to be taken literally by turning ourselves into blocks of wood or stone. It means abstention from action dictated by impure motives involving love, hatred and all other pairs of opposites, but not from the actions necessary for responding to the needs of the moment. This conception of non-action is close to the Taoistic conception of 'wu wei'. In response to hunger, we eat, but this should be done without gluttony, fastidiousness, etc. Similarly, in these days, most people, especially those with families to support, have to work; but each job should be done for its own sake without dwelling upon the profit or loss likely to accrue, and without zest or aversion for particular aspects of the work.

[18] Elsewhere in this text I have sometimes translated 'ting' as 'samādhi', but the trio 'chieh ting hui' is generally translated 'discipline, concentration and wisdom'.

[19] Purity means something much more than the moral purity normally implied by this term in English; it means freedom from ALL attachment and discrimination whatsoever; it would be marred by attachment to good as much as by attachment to bad.

[20] When memory and reverie are cut off, past and future cease to exist. The present does, of course, exist in a firmer sense than either of the others, but it is not PRESENT except when thought of in relation to past and future. The state of mind of an Illumined man is independent of time-relationships.

[21] Literally, 'realization of "the patient endurance of the Uncreate" (anutpattikadharmakśānti)'. The meaning of this Sanskrit Mahāyāna term is 'the patient endurance entailed in resting in the imperturbable Reality beyond birth and death'. The Prajñāpāramitā Śāstra defines it as imperturbably abiding with unflinching faith in the Bhūtatathatā which is free from relativity and subject neither to creation nor destruction'.

[22] The Dharmakāya is that aspect of the Buddhas (and, did they but realize it, of sentient beings) in which they are undifferentiated from the Absolute. Hence it cannot really be divisible into five kinds. The five different names given in the text are

names for the one Dharmakāya as seen in relation to five different functions or from five points of view.

[23] Dharma-Nature is a way of translating the Sanskrit term Dharmatā, which refers to the nature underlying all things and is therefore closely related in meaning to, if not identical with, the word Bhūtatathatā. This vitally important Mahāyāna concept seems to be scarcely known in Hīnayāna Buddhism—though, so I think I have heard, it is not completely unknown.

[24] This must surely mean the Dharmakāya pure and simple, no longer seen from various viewpoints.

[25] This refers to the five thousand conceited bhikṣus mentioned in the Lotus Sūtra. Having attained the relative Nirvāṇa at which the Hīnayānists are said to aim, they refused to listen to the Buddha's sermon and withdrew.   •

[26] A devakanyā or apsara is a kind of minor goddess gifted with a beautiful voice.

[27] The fifty-first stage in the development of a Bodhisattva into a Buddha.

[28] The fifty-second stage of the same.

[29] The three poisons to which primordial ignorance gives rise are wrong desire, anger or passion, and an individual's ignorance of his true nature. From these poisons arise in turn all those thoughts and actions which bind us firmly to Saṁsāra's Wheel of rebirth.

[30] Buddhists who turn away from the world and seek refuge in the void are aiming at a state which is not so lofty as that pursued by the followers of the Ch'an (Zen), Vajrayāna and some other schools—a state requiring no turning away from the world, but an acceptance of the world and everything else as Nirvāṇa. This involves a serene contemplation of the flux of ever-changing forms, accompanied by the knowledge that none of them are real (nothing to be perceived) and by a state of mind impervious to their capacity to stain.

[31] I.e. not with minds like blocks of wood or stone, but with minds free from making distinctions between this and that, free from concepts, notions, judgements, evaluations, likes, dislikes and all the rest.

[32] Here we are very close to the heart of the matter. When we say that Nirvāṇa and Saṁsāra are one, we mean that everything is to be perceived both in its real or undifferentiated form and in

its transient, differentiated form without any distinction being made between the two. Those who cling to the void and eschew the everyday world are as much in error as those who cling to objects as objects without perceiving their essential unity. Beginners like ourselves who can only perceive objects as objects must fix our minds as often as possible upon the idea of their essential unity, and thereby prepare for the intuitive understanding that will come later. Contemplation of the movement and shifting composition of sea-waves is a useful symbolical approach; for, not only are the waves and the sea identical in substance, but also a given wave does not preserve its individual identity for a single moment as the water composing it is never for an instant entirely the same; thus, by the time it reaches us from a distance, every drop it contains will be other than the drops composing it when we saw it first. On the other hand, sea-water is sea-water and the wave is entirely composed of that. Each wave is void—a mere fluctuating appearance identical in substance with every other wave and with the entire ocean; yet it can capsize a boat and is, therefore, intensely real from an ordinary man's point of view. In that sense, it does possess a transient individuality and is thus non-void while retaining its essential voidness.

[33] In the Chinese text the word 'chao' is used both for 'reflect' in the first analogy and for 'shine' in the second.

[34] Maitreya is the name of the Bodhisattva who is expected to become a Buddha and preach to the beings of the era immediately following our own.

[35] The doctrine of annihilation, which implies the previous birth or creation of the thing annihilated, is opposed by Buddhists of all schools. The waves of the sea rise and fall without anything being added to or subtracted from the sea. Forms may come and go, but the marvellous substance of reality is neither augmented nor reduced; nothing is created or born; nothing ceases to be.

[36] Ignorance and everything that proceeds therefrom is exhaustible, whereas wisdom and the reality which is seen by wisdom's light is inexhaustible.

[37] Unwholesome phenomena means those phenomena which are conditioned causally and therefore transient. Wholesome phenomena are unconditioned and permanent.

[38] A leaking mind is a mind constantly losing the truth which it is unable to contain, that is to say a deluded mind still adhering to Saṁsāra's round. The term leaking may also refer to outflows,

i.e. those reactions which occur as a result of the mind's being stained by attachments.

[39] See note 19.

[40] The Mahāyānists frequently use the term Buddha more or less as a synonym for the Absolute, and it is in this sense that the Great Pearl often employs it; but here the word is used with its more widespread meaning of an Enlightened One who, after Illumination, preaches to sentient beings.

[41] Teaching means preaching the Dharma according to the Scriptures; Transmission means preaching or conveying an intuitive understanding of truths discovered through direct experience, and is therefore independent of Scriptures. In some cases, Transmission can take place in silence, as when the Lord Buddha picked a flower and held it up for his disciples to see, whereupon Kāśyapa, traditionally the first Ch'an (Zen) patriarch, smiled his understanding of the truth conveyed by that gesture.

[42] 'Yu wei' and 'wu wei' are terms first used by Taoist sages; they are very hard to translate. Activity and non-activity (in the sense of no calculated activity) are words which suggest only one aspect of their full meaning. Here they are used with the broad meaning of 'worldly' and 'transcendental', i.e. 'pertaining to the realm of transient phenomena' and 'pertaining to eternal reality'.

[43] A Buddha gains Nirvāṇa at the time of his Enlightenment and Parinirvāṇa at the time when he abandons the physical body obtained before Enlightenment. The whole passage means that, from the beginning of his quest to the end of his life, the Lord Buddha never rejected the phenomenal world or regarded his achievement of Nirvāṇa as something attained; for, as Nirvāṇa and Saṁsāra are two aspects of the same ever-present reality, there is nothing to reject and nothing to attain—Enlightenment is an experience of the mind which reveals that which we have always been from the first.

[44] Some Buddhists believe in the existence of actual hells, as states in which people with a large store of evil karma suffer until their evil karma is worked off, but they are never regarded as places of ETERNAL torment! Others regard the word hell as a figure of speech denoting all the sufferings in this life or any other which result from evil karma.

[45] Two apparent contradictions are involved in this series of questions and answers—there is hell and there is not; the Buddha-Nature does not enter and yet it does enter. Ch'an Masters like

the Great Pearl often employ this kind of seeming paradox to illustrate the mean inclusive of both positive and negative. Those whose minds have been freed from stain can no longer be burdened by their karma, however evil, for they have transcended the phenomenal world and reached a point where such opposites as pleasure and suffering are no longer meaningful; moreover, they no longer possess a transient individuality (which alone is capable of suffering). The Buddha-Nature does not enter hell, in that the infinite cannot be contained in the finite; on the other hand, that which enters hell shares the Buddha-Nature common to all; so in that sense the Buddha-Nature does enter hell. (It should be remembered, however, that attempts at logical explanations of Zen paradoxes such as this one do not REALLY advance us much further towards the truth; their deep inner meaning will be apparent only when Illumination is obtained.)

⁴⁶ The words translated 'formation and destruction' are 'ch'êng huai', which render the Sanskrit terms 'vivarta and saṁvarta'. In the Mahāyāna, a cycle of existence is conceived of in four stages—formation (vivarta), existence (vivarta-siddha), destruction (saṁvarta) and void (saṁvarta-siddha).

⁴⁷ I.e. the five types of consciousness connected with our bodily sense organs, together with intellect (manovijñāna), discriminating consciousness (kliṣṭa-manovijñāna) which leads to thinking in terms of self and other, etc., and the storehouse consciousness (ālayavijñāna) from which the seeds or germs of the other types of consciousness spring forth.

⁴⁸ The four Buddha-Wisdoms are listed and explained in the next few paragraphs of the text. For a very full and clear exposition of their meaning see the Lama Govinda's *Foundations of Tibetan Mysticism*, published by Rider and Co.

⁴⁹ As explained in the Introduction, Trikāya denotes the Threefold Body of a Buddha (and, potentially, of all sentient beings). The Dharmakāya is that aspect of a Buddha in which he is one with the Absolute; the Sambhogakāya or Reward Body is that spiritual state in which, though not concrete, a Buddha is seen to possess individual characteristics (like a figure seen in a dream); the Nirmāṇakāya or Body of Transformation is the body, as concrete as those of other sentient beings, which a Buddha employs in order to accomplish the liberation of others. Naturally, the distinctions between one body and another are only relative.

⁵⁰ Correct sensation with regard to the object contemplated is one of the many interpretations of samādhi.

[51] 'The basically impermanent' is a translation of the difficult term 'wu chu pên'. Since objects have no individual nature of their own, they are impermanent; they make their transient appearance only in response to concurrent causes and cease when those causes cease. Thus everything is rooted in impermanence, including the concept of the Trikāya. The true substance and nature of the Trikāya pertain to the permanent, in which the concepts 'three' and 'bodies' have no validity.

[52] The real Buddha-Body is, of course, not a BODY at all, nor divisible into two or three. It is Reality, the Formless, the Unconditioned, the Dharmakāya with the other two kāya absorbed into it.

[53] In fact, we have never been apart from the real Buddhakāya, but we cannot be conscious of it while we remain blinded by delusion.

[54] Here the term Buddha is synonymous with Buddhakāya, the Absolute.

[55] See note 42.

[56] The five skandhas are said to be the components of that which seems to be our ego. Their Sanskrit names are rūpa, vedanā, sañjña, saṁskāra and vijñāna. Form means any form, mental or material, which enters our field of consciousness. Sensation means instantaneous awareness of those forms whereby we 'take them into ourselves'. Then follows perception of their varied nature which leads to impulses (volitions) based upon our evaluation of each form as good or evil, pleasant or unpleasant. Consciousness is the name given to the sum of those mental activities and individual mental characteristics which arise and remain as a result of this process.

[57] I.e. those influences which fan the passions—gain and loss, defamation and eulogy, praise and ridicule, sorrow and joy.

[58] Upon the advice of my friend, the late Pun In-dat, I have corrected what seems to be an error in the block-print by changing 'ling shou-chung shêng' to 'ling-na shou-shêng'. In any case, the meaning is quite clear from the context.

[59] See note 7.

[60] The list of ten evils varies slightly in different Mahāyāna texts. However, there are always three of body, four of speech and three of mind. The variation usually occurs in the speech-category.

⁶¹ This negative approach to the ten virtues indicates that, when the higher stages of the path are reached, clinging to virtue as something positive is as much an obstacle as clinging to evil.

⁶² This refers to the middle of passage number 7 in the text.

⁶³ I.e. thoughts concerned with Buddha, Dharma, Sangha, rules of conduct, almsgiving and merit. Though some Teachers advise their disciples to entertain these thoughts as often as possible, ultimately they must be discarded, together with every other sort of conceptual thinking.

⁶⁴ Abstention from thought does not mean trance-like dullness, but a brilliantly clear state of mind in which the details of every phenomenon are perceived, yet without evaluation or attachment.

⁶⁵ In other words, we have from the first always been potential Buddhas.

⁶⁶ The difference between an Illumined being and an unillumined being is not a difference of nature, but only of success or failure in apprehending the nature common to all.

⁶⁷ According to the Mahāyāna, Nirvāṇa and Saṁsāra (the state in which we are subject to defilement by kleśa) are indivisible. Therefore there is no such thing as quitting Saṁsāra in order to enter Nirvāṇa.

⁶⁸ The lion, being fearless, is often used as a symbol of the Buddha.

⁶⁹ This passage is reminiscent of the discovery by modern physicists that matter consists entirely of energy and that energy, despite the many forms in which it appears, is basically one.

⁷⁰ The samādhi of universality, if translated more literally, would be rendered as the samādhi of one act. In this one act the powers of body, speech and mind are conjoined. Therefore, the general idea is that of holding to one course. It is a samādhi entailing the realization that the nature of all the Buddhas is identical.

⁷¹ Perception does not cease, but there is no longer any division between perceiver and perceiving, or between perceiving and the object perceived.

⁷² By our worldly standards, a Buddha is a rare enough figure. Many Buddhists believe that no Buddha has appeared in the world for about two and a half millenniums. However, they also believe in an infinite number of world-systems and in an infinitude of

aeons; hence, even if only one Buddha were to appear in each world during each aeon, their number would still be as uncountable as grains of dust.

[73] The expression 'other Buddhas' reminds us that, could we but see ourselves as we really are, we should know that we, too, are Buddhas.

[74] Bodhikāya, Buddhakāya and Dharmakāya are all synonyms, any of which may be used according to which of these terms best suits a given context. Literally Bodhikāya means Body of Enlightenment.

[75] Kaliyug is the name given to the present era, namely the era of decline in our understanding of the Dharma.

[76] Rāhula, the son of Śākyamuni Buddha, is sometimes regarded as the originator of esoteric Buddhism.

[77] 'Ultimate' is used in this and the preceding passages in the sense of 'absolute'—a term which the Great Pearl uses sparingly for fear it should be taken to imply its own opposite, 'relative', and thereby occasion dualistic thinking.

[78] Here is a reminder that the void is not nothingness, but a marvellous substance devoid of own-characteristics and yet capable of manifesting every kind of form.

[79] This is a reference to those passages in the Diamond and Lotus Sūtras which speak of the Buddhas as predicting the future attainment of Buddhahood by their disciples. E.g. the Buddha Dīpaṁkara predicted Śākyamuni's attainment of Buddhahood.

[80] A reference to a fundamental Ch'an tenet taken from the Diamond Sūtra, which states that the Tathāgata attained nothing by his Enlightenment and that he had no Dharma which could be preached. This means that Enlightenment, instead of altering our state, discloses to us what we have always been; and that the inner truth of the Dharma is inexpressible in words. Therefore the Tathāgata made use of relative truths for the sake of unenlightened beings.

[81] Chien Chou, now called Chien Ou, is in Fukien Province.

[82] 'Go and take a rest' is a Ch'an idiom meaning 'You should set your minds at rest'. The Chinese wording contains the idea of 'Go to yourself', so the saying is a direct pointing at the mind.

[83] The moon stands for enlightenment and the pond-water for self-nature. The implication is: 'How can enlightenment be caught?'

[84] Another direct pointing to their minds which were facing the pond.

[85] A monk's way of saying 'I'.

[86] See note 80.

[87] Here, as so often, the word Tathāgata is used with a dual meaning, or at least with a meaning open to either of two interpretations, since they amount to the same—(1) the Buddha Śākyamuni (Gautama) as the embodiment of the Suchness; (2) the Suchness or Absolute itself.

[88] There is a common, somewhat pantheistic, belief found among the adherents of many religions, including not a few Mahāyānists, that 'everything is One'. The Great Pearl is at pains to show that this is only true in a qualified sense. He distinguishes more than once between sentient beings and insentient matter. To him, as to most Ch'an followers, the only reality is Mind; sentient beings one and all partake of that Mind, whereas all that has form (including, of course, the physical characteristics of sentient beings) is an illusory creation of Mind. Whatever is illusory, such as plants and rocks, cannot share the Buddha-Nature or self-nature which pertains only to Mind, and therefore to sentient beings in that their real selves are identical with Mind.

[89] The Master is pointing directly at Mind, which is all-embracing and omnipresent.

[90] Fa Ming had mistaken the Chinese equivalent of Siddam (the Sanskrit alphabet) for a term meaning Sarvathasiddha (one who has realized every desire, also the given name of Śākyamuni).

[91] These are the three divisions of the Buddhist Canon—(1) sermons ascribed to the Buddha himself; (2) the monastic rules; (3) commentaries, philosophical and metaphysical works composed by others.

[92] This question was meant to catch out the Great Pearl, as not one Buddhist in ten thousand would know or attach importance to the answer. Amitābha Buddha is viewed as the embodiment of Infinite Compassion and Boundless Light; he has seldom been regarded as a historical personage. The Great Pearl's prompt answer testifies to his immense learning. Ch'an Masters do not just dispense with books from the beginning, as some people in the West seem inclined to think. They dispense with books when they have acquired sufficient preliminary knowledge to be able to transcend writings by direct experience. It is not surprising that Fa Ming was impressed by this unexpected display of learning.

[93] The three poisons are: (wrong) desire, anger and ignorance. The three cumulative precepts are: (1) the formal sets of five, eight and ten precepts common to all Buddhist schools; (2) whatever works for compassion; (3) whatever works for the liberation of sentient beings. (2) and (3) may also be regarded as extensions of each of the ten precepts in (1). For example, by not killing we show compassion and we do not interfere with a life-span tending towards deliverance.

[94] The Northern Ch'an School, which died out in China a few centuries after the establishment of the Ch'an School, believed in gradual Enlightenment. The Southern Ch'an School, also known as the Hui Nêng School or Southern School, emphasizes the sudden nature of Enlightenment, and it is this which forms the central thesis of the Great Pearl's teaching.

[95] When an Illuminated man eats or sleeps, unlike a worldling who constantly indulges in discrimination, he does not discriminate at all.

[96] This is a reference to the gāthā chanted by the Eighteenth Indian Patriarch, Gayasata, when he transmitted the Dharma of Mind to the Nineteenth Patriarch, Kumarata:

> The self-existing seed in ground of Mind,
> According with concurrent cause, sprouts forth.
> Concurrent cause and sprout no mutual hindrance raise,
> For that which is produced is not producible.

It is also written in the gāthā chanted by Tao Hsin, the Fourth Chinese Patriarch, when he transmitted the Dharma of Mind to Hung Jên, the Fifth Patriarch:

> Growth is latent in the seed
> Which sprouts when planted in causal ground.
> This great cause unites with nature
> At the time of growth—yet nothing grows.

[97] Aśvaghoṣa was the author of many important Mahāyāna works, notably *The Śāstra of the Awakening of Faith* (Ch'i Hsin Lun).

[98] That the Dharmakāya becomes manifest in response to the needs of men indicates that the Buddha must wait for opportunities to perform the work of salvation. Sentient beings have first to make themselves capable of 'being ferried across to Nirvāṇa's shore' by practising the Dharma, performing all virtuous actions and, above all, by lifting themselves above the realm of relativities. As the Diamond Sūtra points out, it is by the practice of the Dharma that roots are developed which make salvation possible.

The Buddhas and Bodhisattvas are not gods who can pluck anyone or everyone from the realm of causality without those people making an immense effort. When Śākyamuni Buddha walked the earth, he could not save those who, like his cousin Devadatta, did not believe in his doctrine. Some Western scholars have lauded Buddhism as a religion which does not involve faith; no Asian Buddhists, Ch'an, Mahāyāna or Theravādin, would agree with them. Faith is an essential quality, but it should not be blind faith, for the efficacy of the Dharma can be tested at each level.

⁹⁹ As will be seen in section 14 of Book II, there is a sense in which an Illumined man may speak of bamboos and flowers as the Dharmakāya and as Prajñā, if that is expedient; but for an unenlightened man to go around saying 'Everything is the Dharmakāya; everything is nothing but Prajñā' is meaningless. It is only in a certain sense that we can equate a manifestation with that which manifests it. Sun and sunlight, for example, are not in every sense the same, though we should be hard put to it to draw a sharp distinction between them.

¹⁰⁰ This refers to men who know the sūtras by heart but who neglect practice and training.

¹⁰¹ Mind IS the Buddha, but we should CLING to nothing, for clinging to a truth involves us in the dualism of excluding its opposite. Those who have attained to a silent recognition of their own-nature do not retain concepts of its being or not being this or that. The term 'devils', which is stronger than any of those used to describe other categories of deluded people, perhaps implies that to have come so close to the truth and then gone astray is worse than being merely stupid and ignorant.

¹⁰² A Ch'an idiom meaning those who are indifferent to externals and do not seek them.

¹⁰³ Buddha, Dharma and Saṅgha are commonly taken to mean the Buddha, the Doctrine and the Order of Monks; to some they mean the Absolute, Universal Law, and the order of Bodhisattvas and Arahants; but to adepts like the Great Pearl they mean Three Aspects of One Truth. Incidentally, the Vajrayānists (Lamaists) take the Three Jewels to mean Guru, Deva, Ḍākinī—terms which have the esoteric meaning of the Buddha as the Guru, the Buddha as Transcendent Reality, and the Buddha as Reality within ourselves. This comes close to the Ch'an definition, which is not surprising because, though the two schools appear so dissimilar, they are particularly close in essentials.

¹⁰⁴ This is the principle sūtra of the Hua Yen (Kegon) School.

[105] A Ch'an idiom meaning: 'Look into that which makes you stand here for so long; go away and take good care of your minds.'

[106] A Ch'an idiom meaning: 'My mind has caused me to come here to sit face to face with your minds,' i.e. to reveal the presence of mind wherever someone may happen to be. This is another of the Great Pearl's direct pointings to the mind.

[107] I.e., just go and set your minds at rest.

[108] I.e., why doubt about your Self?

[109] This is a reference to the Lotus Sūtra, in which it says that five thousand bhikṣus who thought they had attained final Nirvāṇa refused to listen to the Buddha's sermon and withdrew.

[110] Literally: '. . . Gates of Prajñā which reveal the voidness of the three-wheel condition of all almsgiving (dāna).'

[111] The One Vehicle is the Buddha Vehicle as contrasted with the three vehicles of the śrāvakas, pratyeka-buddhas and Bodhi-sattvas.

[112] I.e., I have relinquished all attachments to location (or) my mind does not abide anywhere—so where can I gather people?

[113] I.e., mind is speechless, how can it urge people to do anything? In this and the preceding sentence, 'this old monk' has the outward meaning of 'I' and the inner meaning of 'mind'.

[114] If he understood himself, he would thereby divide his undivided whole into subject and object. The Master tried his best to teach his visitor, but the latter seemed unable to extract the profound meaning from his words.

[115] Prajñā is free from all discrimination.

[116] In the Vimalakīrti Nirdeśa Sūtra it is related that when Subhūti, one of the Buddha's disciples, knocked at Vimalakīrti's door and asked for food, the Upāsaka spoke those words to instruct his visitor. Usually, Buddhist monks avoid heretics to keep themselves from being drawn into heresies; they praise those giving alms and regard them as owners of 'fields of blessedness'; they cling to the idea that those making offerings to monks will never fall into the three evil states of existence; they revere the Buddha and protect the Dharma; and they join the Order in the hope of attaining liberation. At the ordinary level of relativities, all these ideas and deeds are admirable, but they are relativities. The development of a universal mind, which alone can enable them to reach their goal, is above such dualities. Vimalakīrti's

words implied that he thought Subhūti sufficiently advanced to begin to rise above all concepts involving duality; for, otherwise, he would not succeed in his quest for Bodhi. The six heretics are the six senses; though they constantly mislead us, we cannot get away from them to find the Absolute elsewhere. In other words, we should realize the Absolute from the very midst of relativities and contraries.

[117] I.e., because of attachment to the reality of an ego and its objects.

[118] These are the two kinds of food mentioned in the Lotus Sūtra.

[119] The question was asked with reference to what was said in Passage 19 of Book I.

[120] Compare with St John's Gospel—'In the beginning was the Word . . .' The Bīja-Mantras of the Vajrayānists are used in this symbolic way.

[121] After the ascension of the Prince of Chi State to the throne, the minister appointed by him ruled the people so badly that the situation rapidly deteriorated. A new minister appointed to take his place, after upbraiding the Prince with the words referred to here, served him loyally and restored the country's prosperity.

[122] A reference to a passage in the Vimalakīrti Nirdeśa Sūtra— 'Mañjuśrī said to Vimalakīrti: "We have all spoken about entry into the non-dual Dharma-gate to Enlightenment. Virtuous One, it is now your turn to enlighten us on a Bodhisattva's entry into the non-dual Dharma-Gate." Vimalakīrti remained silent. There-upon, Mañjuśrī praised him, saying: "Excellent, excellent! That which is beyond expression in verbal and written words is the real entry into the non-dual Dharma-Gate." '

[123] There are ten stages of a Bodhisattva's development into Buddhahood.

[124] The Vinaya Master was discriminating and could not be awakened to that Absolute state which is perceptible only to those who have realized the Buddha-Wisdom.

[125] An asamkhyeya kalpa denotes an uncountable number of aeons. Three of them are sometimes said to be required for a Bodhisattva's development into a Buddha.

[126] Here 'Way' (Tao) is used for the mind. The Master's parting words indicate that it was his visitor's mind which caused him to stride away.

[127] A stirless mind may perceive visions of Buddhas and demons created by the five aggregates. For this reason, the inner wisdom should be developed and used to look into these visions; then, as the Enlightened Masters put it: 'Its indestructible sword should be used to cut down Buddhas, should Buddhas appear, and to cut down demons, should demons appear.'

[128] This is the meditation according to the 'Perfect Teaching' of the T'ien T'ai School and derives from Nāgārjuna's Śāstra on the Prajñāpāramitā Sūtra: it explains the doctrine set forth by that śāstra of 'One mind and its three aspects of wisdom'. The practice is intended for those with sharp roots (a high degree of spirituality). It is taught that contemplation of one aspect of wisdom involves simultaneous contemplation of all three of its aspects. The three characteristics of illusory existence—creation, abiding and destruction—are thereby simultaneously transmuted into the three aspects of wisdom. The same result is achieved through the T'ien T'ai threefold meditative study of the void, the unreal and the mean. This 'Perfect Teaching' of the T'ien T'ai School contrasts with the gradual methods of those schools which differentiate between various aspects and stages of Truth.

[129] Chih Chê is the Fourth Patriarch of the T'ien T'ai School.

[130] Illusions based on concepts of existence or non-existence inevitably depend on attachment to one of four beliefs: (1) that everything has permanent existence; (2) that nothing has permanent existence; (3) that the ego (soul), but not the body, has permanent existence; (4) that the ego, unlike the body, is not impermanent. These are tersely expressed in Chinese by the famous four sets of concepts derived from the Indian Buddhist logicians: (1) existence; (2) non-existence; (3) both existence and non-existence; (4) neither existence nor non-existence. They have been interpreted in various ways but, in any case, all interpretations of any of the four involve attachments to concepts unacceptable to Ch'an and some other forms of Mahāyāna Buddhism.

[131] The questions show that the questioner had got as far as understanding that immaterial things may be big and small at the same time; otherwise the second question would scarcely have followed the answer to the first; but the Great Pearl wished to wipe out altogether the duality inherent in such thinking. Prajñā is omnipresent, but not to be thought of in terms of space. When the great English poet proclaimed that the whole universe is contained in a single flower, he expressed a truth perhaps even deeper than the one intended; for, since the Absolute is non-

spacial, a single grain of dust can contain not PART of it but the whole. But then, perhaps that is exactly what the poet meant; Buddhists have no monopoly of intuitive understanding.

[132] In that sūtra it is related that the Upāsaka Vimalakīrti asked some visiting Bodhisattvas to relate the means by which they had entered the non-dual Dharma-Gate. When they had explained how they had done this by wiping out all dual concepts, such as those relating to 'I' and 'other than I', Mañjuśrī expressed the opinion that entrance through that door consisted in 'neither words nor speech, in neither indicating nor knowing, and in neither questioning nor answering with regard to all dharmas (phenomena, doctrines, etc.) whatsoever'. When Vimalakīrti was asked in his turn, he remained silent, saying nothing. Thus the Bodhisattvas used words and speech to reveal non-dual or Ablute Reality; Mañjuśrī revealed it through absence of words and speech; while Vimalakīrti revealed it by maintaining a perfect silence, thus wiping out the duality of words and speech on the one hand and the concept of their absence on the other.

[133] Pên t'i (fundamental substance) and chi yung (manifesting function) are terms meaning approximately the same as t'i (substance) and yung (function).

[134] The Absolute Dharmakāya is the undivided whole resulting from the integration of principle and activity, of the fundamental and its manifestation.

[135] This presents the Ch'an teaching which consists of first integrating the two denominations into one undivided whole, and then wiping out the conception of One, thereby overcoming the last subtle attachment in order to realize the Absolute, which is neither a unity nor a plurality.

[136] This means that if, in your quest for eternity, you allow yourself to discriminate between the two aspects of time, today and tomorrow, that is like discriminating between the mind that causes you to wear a robe, eat, walk, stand, sit or recline and the mind you want to realize for the perception of self-nature and the attainment of Buddhahood.

[137] This commentary derives its name from that of the monastery where Tao Yin, the commentator, lived.

[138] The three insights are the powers arising from the universal insight of the Buddha into all that has happened in past lives, is happening now and will happen in the future. There are various

K

lists of the six transcendental powers—they are those siddhis which arise as a by-product of sustained right meditation, but which some people mistakenly (and dangerously) choose for their main goal.

[139] There are many stories of divine responses; their purpose is to exhort people to recite the sūtras regularly and to practise good works.

[140] In China, according to the lore of Fêng Shui or geomancy, the position of ancestral tombs greatly influences the fortunes of the descendants.

[141] Most phenomena have a visible form and a name. Does the form come to mind before or after the name? Does speech precede or succeed silence? The monk was enquiring how to interpret them correctly in order to integrate these pairs and thereby eliminate the time element.

[142] A direct pointing to the mind, which could be perceived through its function of speaking during their dialogue.

[143] The dry, unfertilized stage of wisdom (i.e. unfertilized by the Buddha-Truth), otherwise called worldly wisdom, is the first of the ten stages common to the three Vehicles.

[144] There are some Hīnayānists who shun the world as being evil and who cultivate forms of meditation leading to something very much like blankness of mind.

[145] The Sambhogakāya is one of the Trikāya or Three Bodies which have been briefly discussed in the Introduction.

[146] The Master wiped out the dualisms involved in 'to do' and 'not to do', 'right' and 'wrong', in order to reveal the Absolute Dharmakāya which is incomparable, inconceivable and indivisible.

[147] The questioner was to be blamed for stirring his mind and discriminating between man, boat and shell-fish, which were all creations of his own discriminating mind and could not have real existence in the Absolute Suchness. This direct pointing at the mind runs throughout the text, which cannot be understood except in that context.

[148] When teaching their disciples, Ch'an Masters used to point directly to mind which is stirred by worldly feelings and passions and by its surroundings. This was done according to circumstances by speech, silence, gestures, expressions and so forth.

¹⁴⁹ A quotation from the Vimalakīrti Nirdeśa Sūtra. Vimala-kīrti addressed these words to Mañjuśrī. 'Impermanence' here translates 'wu chu' (non-abiding). See note 47.

¹⁵⁰ The disciples of the Buddha began to practise the Hīnayāna teaching and clung to an abiding place in the relative Nirvāṇa. Later, when initiated into the Mahāyāna, they were disturbed by the concept of the voidness of things. Thus, advancing further, they did not gain any new experience and, looking back, they found they had lost their old abode. Confronted by the void, they felt scared.

¹⁵¹ I.e., cannot be reached by your mind which is the very source of your words. This implies that a person's mind can reach the inexpressible beyond the reach of words.

¹⁵² A seed-nature or germ-nature means a nature which can sprout and develop from the essential nature.

¹⁵³ Dhāraṇī means absolute control over good and evil passions and influences.

¹⁵⁴ The Non-Abiding Nirvāṇa is the fourth of the four kinds or stages of Nirvāṇa. The Buddha does not abide in Final Nirvāṇa, for his compassion leads him to convert and liberate those still in Saṁsāra.

¹⁵⁵ I.e., a ring of fire drawn by a circling torch.

¹⁵⁶ I.e., for ritual purposes.

¹⁵⁷ The Master was pointing directly at the mind which embodies the Buddha-Dharma.

¹⁵⁸ I.e., what the Master had just said, referring to mind which is neither within nor without nor yet between the two, was very clear indeed.

¹⁵⁹ Everyone's mind is fundamentally that of a Buddha and can actually reach Buddhahood by purification from all stirrings and attachments.

¹⁶⁰ The Buddha-Nature is beyond hell and cannot suffer. This seems to contradict one of the Master's statements in passage 28 of Book I, but it will be remembered that he immediately contradicted that statement in the same passage. The seeming contradiction is explained in note 45.

¹⁶¹ The Great Sūtra or Great Book is another term for Mind or Wisdom.

[162] The Sixth Indian Patriarch Miccaka chanted the following gāthā when he transmitted the Dharma of Mind to the Seventh Patriarch Vasumitra:

> There is neither mind nor realization,
> While that which can be realized is not the Dharma.
> It is only when the mind is seen to be unreal
> That the Dharma of all minds can be truly understood.

[163] The last two sentences mean: 'There is not a thing which can be of real concern to you, for all things are but illusions. Take good care of your minds, which should not be stirred, so that you can realize Mind and perceive your self-nature.'

CHINESE TERMS IN THE TEXT OFFERING
SPECIAL DIFFICULTIES

HSIN, mind, heart. This terms occurs constantly in the text, sometimes with the meaning of 'his mind', 'your mind', etc., and sometimes with the meaning of MIND, which is in fact synonymous with Reality, the Absolute and so on. It is also employed to denote the uses to which mind is put, approximately in the sense of 'to think', 'to be cognizant of', 'to be aware' and so on. It can therefore mean Mind, someone's mind, mental processes, thought, thoughts, etc.; or it may have its basic Chinese meaning, which is 'heart'; moreover, even when it means mind, it includes much of what Westerners mean by heart. It has overtones and undertones close in meaning to such words as the subconscious, the subliminal mind and (in a manner of speaking) the soul. The character HSIN may sometimes suggest several of these meanings simultaneously; the frequent omission of any personal pronoun in the Chinese text is often intended to bring home the identity of 'our minds' with MIND.

FA, Dharma or dharma. Dharma may be used as a synonym for the Absolute, for the Law of the Universe, for Buddhist Doctrine, for Right Belief and Right Action and so on. Without a capital D, dharma(s) means any or every kind of phenomena—things, ideas, forces, the constituent parts of things, the infinitesimal 'moments' which combine to form a single flash of thought, the atom-like units of which the Theravādin Buddhists believe phenomena to be composed and so on ad infinitum. The Great Pearl employs FA in some of the above senses, but also in its purely Chinese sense to mean a method or as a sort of suffix which can sometimes be omitted. In general, throughout this book, I have used a capital D wherever the word means something like Universal Law of the Buddha's Doctrine and a small d wherever it means something like 'things'. Wherever necessary, I have included an English translation in brackets.

TAO, way or path. In this book, it is not used precisely in its Taoistic sense as the Force or Spirit governing and pervading the universe, except in the Dialogues where a Taoist is speaking; but it is often employed abstractedly to mean the Way of the Buddhas, the Way of Enlightenment, the Way of Zen and so on. It is also used more concretely to mean a method, way or path.

WU, illumination, awakening. The Great Pearl employs this word to mean Illumination, Enlightenment, etc., so it is equivalent to the Japanese Satori; but the fact that he also uses other terms for Enlightenment, such as Bodhi and Annuttara-samyak-sambodhi, as well as some Chinese translations of those terms, suggests to me that the initial Illumination which is the real purpose of this book, though identical in kind with Supreme Enlightenment, may differ from it in degree or permanence. The common Japanese use of Satori also seems to suggest something less in degree than Supreme Enlightenment. In some places the Great Pearl also employs WU in a less exalted sense, meaning 'to awaken to', 'to become instantly aware of', etc. I have used Awakening, Illumination or Enlightenment wherever WU is employed in its major sense, and Indian words with the same meaning, such as Bodhi, wherever they occur in the text.

CHIEH T'O, deliverance. The Great Pearl uses this as a synonym for Illumination or, rather, to denote the natural consequence of Illumination; it takes place abruptly, rather in the way that water, after gradually getting hotter, suddenly boils.

CH'AN or CH'AN-NA, dhyāna or meditation, meaning abstention from wrong thinking, i.e. from pluralistic or dualistic thought and so on.

TING or SANWEI or SAMOTI, samādhi, contemplation of our original nature which is uncreate Mind. However, where TING connotes the second component of the three methods of training— discipline, concentration and wisdom—I have translated TING as dhyāna.

CH'AN TING, dhyāna and samādhi.

K'UNG, śūnya, śūnyatā, void, voidness, the void, immaterial, immateriality, etc. This is a conception fundamental to the whole of Mahāyāna Buddhism, though precise definitions of it vary according to school or sect. According to the Ch'an School, only mind is real. It is void, not at all in the sense of being a vacuum, but in the sense that it has no own-characteristics and is, therefore, not discoverable to the senses by shape, size or colour, etc. Phenomena are void in that they are all transient creations of Mind, which possesses the marvellous capability of producing within itself all possible types of phenomena. As mental creations, they are naturally void or immaterial.

T'I and YUNG, substance and function. T'I is the universal mind 'substance', formless, immaterial, imperceptible. YUNG is its function, whereby every kind of phenomenon is or can be produced in response to the needs of sentient beings. When a person acquires this YUNG, he obtains unobstructed use of mind; he becomes fully aware of everything while remaining unstained by anything at all.

HSING, PÊN HSING, TZŬ HSING, original nature, own nature, self-nature. We are taught that all of us possess an identical nature, that of voidness (undifferentiated immateriality). When we are Illumined, we perceive our own nature to be thus; we perceive that we have not and cannot possibly have any other nature, and yet that it is not our own in the sense of mine or yours, in that it belongs to all. Thereupon, the last lingering traces of egotism give place to unlimited compassion for those who still suppose there are things to be gained or lost and who therefore struggle against 'you' or 'him' for a 'me' which is no other than the opposing 'you' or 'him'.

CHIH and HUI, Jñāna and Prajñā, pure consciousness and discerning wisdom. Hui is used sometimes just to mean knowing and understanding things in the ordinary sense of those words, sometimes to mean Prajñā, the Highest Wisdom which reveals to us our own nature, the voidness (immateriality) of what is real and, simultaneously, empowers us to perceive the minutest distinctions of form. The Great Pearl sometimes employs the Indian word Prajñā in the Chinese text where, in some cases, it becomes one of the many synonyms used to distinguish the various aspects of the Absolute, of Reality.

SHÊNG and FAN FU, holy and ordinary (common) people. These terms are used respectively to mean those who are Illumined and those who are not, that is, Buddhas and sentient beings, but it is made clear that there is no real difference between them, since all of them share the same nature; it is only that the SHÊNG or holy ones have realized their own-nature, while the FAN FU or ordinary beings have still to realize it.

GLOSSARY OF SANSKRIT TERMS

(Wherever the Great Pearl departs markedly from the meanings given below, this will be sufficiently clear from the text.)

ACHĀRYĀ, scholar, learned man—a term of respect.

ANUTTARA-SAMYAK-SAMBODHI, see SAMYAK-SAMBODHI.

ASAMSKRTA, not pertaining to the impermanent, wu wei. |

ASURA, a being similar to a Titan or fallen angel.

AVIDYĀ, primordial ignorance, ignorance of our true nature.

BHIKṢU, Buddhist monk, literally beggar.

BHŪTATATHATĀ, the Absolute viewed as the universal womb.

BĪJA-MANTRA, a seed-mantra or exclamation of power consisting of only one word.

BODHI, Enlightenment, full Illumination.

BODHIKĀYA, the Body of the Absolute viewed as the fruit of Enlightenment.

BODHIMAṆḌALA, a place or sphere in which Enlightenment can be obtained.

BODHISATTVA, (1) a future Buddha, (2) a spiritual being who has renounced immediate entrance into Nirvāṇa in order to assist others thereto, (3) a sincere follower of the Way.

BUDDHA, (1) A Being who has achieved Enlightenment, (2) a synonym for the Buddhakāya or Absolute.

BUDDHAKĀYA, the Absolute, viewed as the state of Buddhahood.

DĀNA, (1) alms or gifts bestowed for religious or charitable reasons, (2) relinquishment.

DEVAKANYĀ, a class of minor female divinity.

DHARMA, (1) the Doctrine of the Buddha, (2) Universal Law, (3) a method or way, (4) an entity of any sort—thing, idea, concept, etc.

DHARMA-DHĀTU, the Absolute, i.e. the Dharma-Realm.

DHARMAKĀYA, the Dharma-Body or the Absolute, viewed as the Ultimate Reality with which Buddhas or Enlightened Beings are one and indivisible.

DHYĀNA, deep abstraction into which erroneous thoughts cannot enter, translated into Chinese as Ch'an or Ch'an-na and into Japanese as Zen, from which the Ch'an (Zen) School of Buddhism takes its name.

GĀTHĀ, a verse, usually of a sacred kind.

HĪNAYĀNA, one of the two major divisions of Buddhism; it is prevalent in South-East Asia.

KARMA, the causal process binding every action to preceding and concurrent causes and to the results which must spring from it.

KLEŚA, a defilement, passion, etc.

KṢĀNTI, forbearance.

MAHĀPARINIRVĀṆA, ultimate Nirvāṇa. (Nirvāṇa can be achieved in this life; ultimate Nirvāṇa follows at death.)

MAHĀYĀNA, one of the two major divisions of Buddhism; it is prevalent in the more northerly countries of Asia—China, Tibet, Japan, etc.

NIRMĀṆAKĀYA, The Body of Transformation in which Buddhas and Bodhisattvas take on physical characteristics similar to those of ordinary beings for the purpose of delivering such beings.

NIRVĀṆA, the final state into which beings enter when, becoming Enlightened, they are no longer bound by the consciousness of an illusory ego.

PĀRAMITĀ, a means of crossing to the further shore, thereby entering Nirvāṇa; there are six of them required for this purpose.

PRAJÑĀ, highest wisdom, transcendent wisdom, etc. This term is also employed as a synonym for the universal 'substance'.

PRATYEKA-BUDDHA, a being who achieves Enlightenment on his own and who does not then go forth to preach the Dharma.

PRETA, a hungry, tantalized ghost, led by evil karma into that sad but temporary state of existence.

SAMĀDHI, a state of complete withdrawal of the mind from its surroundings, the fruit of perfectly performed meditation; it consists of pure contemplation of our original nature or mind.

SAṂBHODI, Supreme Enlightenment.

SAMBHOGAKĀYA, the body in which Enlightened Beings enjoy the rewards of liberation from worldly things and in which they can appear to other beings in insubstantial form.

SAMSĀRA, the realm of relativity, transience and illusion, as contrasted with the permanence and quiescence of Nirvāna.

SAMSKRTA, pertaining to the impermanent, yu wei.

SAMYAK-SAMBODHI, Supreme Enlightenment.

ŚĀSTRA, a sacred treatise or else a commentary upon a sūtra.

SIDDHI, supernormal power.

ŚĪLA, the precepts, the morality observed by Buddhists.

SKANDHA, a component of personality; there are five of them.

ŚRĀVAKA, a hearer—one who approaches the Dharma as a result of hearing it preached.

SŪTRA, a volume containing the actual teaching of the Buddha. (This term is only very occasionally used to denote a sacred book of which the authorship is not directly attributed to the Buddha.)

TATHĀGATA, (1) a term used to denote a Buddha, literally the Thus-Come, He-Who-Is-Thus, He-Who-Is-The-Suchness; (2) the Suchness of all Dharmas.

TRIKĀYA, the Triple Body of a Buddha. (See Introduction.)

TRIPITAKA, the entire collection of Buddhist Scriptures.

UPĀSAKA, a layman who lives according to certain strict rules.

VAJRA, literally diamond or adamantine; used in the sense of imperishable, real, ultimate.

VAJRAYĀNA, the school of Mahāyāna Buddhism prevalent in Tibet and Mongolia, commonly called Lamaism in the West, where its doctrines and practices are much misunderstood.

VINAYA, the discipline observed by Buddhist monks.

VĪRYA, zeal.

INDEX